fearing the stigmata

Humorously Holy Stories
of a Young Catholic's Search
for a Culturally Relevant Faith

Matt Weber

LOYOLAPRESS.
A JESUIT MINISTRY
Chicago

LOYOLA PRESS.
A JESUIT MINISTRY

3441 N. Ashland Avenue
Chicago, Illinois 60657
(800) 621-1008
www.loyolapress.com

Cover image courtesy of The CatholicTV® Network.

Library of Congress Cataloging-in-Publication Data
Weber, Matt.
  Fearing the stigmata : humorously holy stories of a young Catholic's search for a culturally relevant faith / Matt Weber.
    p. cm.
  ISBN-13: 978-0-8294-3736-2
  ISBN-10: 0-8294-3736-3
  1. Weber, Matt. 2. Catholics--Biography. I. Title.
  BX4705.W397A3 2012
  282.092—dc23
  [B]

                                                          2012015472

Printed in the United States of America.
12 13 14 15 16 17 Bang 10 9 8 7 6 5 4 3 2 1

To my dear mother, loving father, and two pesky sisters.

contents

introduction

They were blackened, oblong, and curiously placed. Sometimes they appeared circular, other instances just a starkly darkened dot. Sprinkled as strange motifs throughout my Catholic saint picture books, I thought perhaps they were artistic defects, a malfunction of the brush, or errors in print. Yet they persisted. Fed up with this fourth-grade mystery, I waited for religion class that afternoon and appropriately raised my hand with fervent hope for answers.

"Yes, Matthew," said my all-knowing religion teacher at Holy Cross Grammar School.

"Why does my friend St. Francis have spots on his hands and feet?" I asked in prepubescent squeakiness. I remember wondering whether these spots were the result of "leopard-sy" or were caused by some other condition.

"Well, Matthew," she said, "those are holes, and they are called the stigmata, and it reflects the wounds Jesus suffered during his crucifixion."

"How did St. Francis get them?" I asked with queasy curiosity.

"He was good, Matthew, . . . a good Catholic."

That night I went home and decided I had better start doing some more sinning. Nothing too bad—I think I may have pinched my little sister and neglected to put some clothes in the hamper—just enough to make sure I would be stigmata-free that night. While at the time I may not have fully understood the complexity of her answer, my teacher's words have been present in every one of my actions, informing many decisions, providing me with bearings to a faith life I still hold dear.

After all, being Catholic has taught me many things about what happens when we are bad. As children we are told that sinning makes Jesus cry, blackens the soul, and quite simply and scarily, sends you to hell. Conversely, all the lessons of being good point to bliss; heaven, closeness to Jesus, and happiness are all by-products of living a good Catholic life. Yet here I was, a now-confused nine-year-old wondering about this gaping inaccuracy and a possible outcome outlier of being good. Living the life of a "good Catholic" now meant the risk of something extremely painful: waking up one morning to four bloody holes and a dripping chest gash.

If this were to happen, what would I tell my mother? How would I receive communion? It would fall right through my hands! How would this affect my basketball shot? Could I hide these hideous marks? I would have to throw out all my sandals (and hopes of a foot modeling career), and my white T-shirts would need nightly bleaching.

Of course, as I got older I realized the odds of getting the stigmata were slim. But what really plagued me was the question: How good did I really want to be, and at what cost? It is in this paradox that I have been trying to understand the balance of living a good Catholic life into my late twenties, yet also avoiding the stigmata. The road I have taken brings me to church every Sunday, my brown hair floating in a sea of gray and white hair. I often go alone, have no children, and am usually seen three quarters of the way in the back of the church, end of a pew, dressed in jeans. I am not a seminarian, nor do I feel a calling to that life (regardless of my grandfather's wishes). I sing occasionally, fully genuflect 80 percent of the time, and try not to keep my feet on the kneelers when I sit. I think about leaving after communion to catch the beginning of the football game but usually think otherwise, as the silent echoes of my mother and countless nuns remind me of my priorities. If you look around church this Sunday, you'll likely see one of me. We are often thought of as a rare breed, perhaps on the Catholic "endangered species" list, but a resilient troop.

Yet, there always is that tension. How holy do I want to be? How comfortable am I to be "marked" by my Catholic faith? Am I willing to stand out—not just with my height because I am almost 6'4"? Rather, am I ready to be known as a Catholic, and not just in my home or my parish or Catholic school? I had to ask myself if I was ready to be more public with my faith and even take to the airwaves for what I believe.

I am a twenty-seven-year-old Catholic male. I love the Virgin Mary more than mushroom pizzas, sometimes play blues harmonica with the church choir, smuggle in ice-cream sundaes to cloistered nuns, and started my own Catholic television show. I submit to you this story of how I have tried to be a good Catholic all my life, in constant pursuit of staying holy but avoiding ever being truly holey.

1

talking to statues

At the busy intersection of Market Street and North Beacon, she waited for me. I was never late, and she was always happy to visit. These kinds of relationships are rare in life, and this was one I sincerely valued and held in respect. Our meeting place was three-quarters of the way up the steep Market Street hill. My legs would rest as my mouth would race. She was a great listener, as I did most of the talking. She was masterful at calming me down, sharing in my joys, and just rehashing the detritus of a day.

This woman is one of my best friends in the entire world, and her name is Mary. While she does not comment on my Facebook photos or text me Red Sox score updates at night, we have other ways to communicate. For two years, my favorite form has been our roadside chats.

Our evening chats were my idea, but there were a few complications. I am by no means a private person, but I am fairly reserved when it comes to public signs of faith. I know that often public displays of any faith can make people uncomfortable, so I try to minimize this. As I gingerly parked my bicycle for the first time in front of this shrine, I quickly decided that it was silly to fear the blank stares of confused car passengers. While they were likely expecting to see more wrinkles on this resting pilgrim, I decided to invite myself over. For me, the desire to both rest and reflect after a long day's work halfway up a daunting Boston hill superseded any oversensitivity about the opinions of onlookers. So, there I sat.

As the sun slowly set and I rested on a cold granite bench, I started talking out loud to Mary. Now, usually in church, prayer is done formally with the community or privately to oneself. It is often rehearsed, memorized, and catechetically established. Yet, here I found myself in extemporaneous prayer, asking Mary questions, telling her jokes, and complaining about everything from the burnt pizza at lunch to the strange rash on my arm. I had never really prayed like this before, and I was wondering, on many levels, if it was OK. Was it acceptable to pray like this? Does it count as prayer? Can I treat Mary like a friend? Is this irreverent in some way? Am I scaring the locals with fears of a loitering paranoid schizophrenic engaging in a conversation with a stiff albino giant?

After a few days of being ignored by onlookers and passing cars, I began to feel more comfortable in this type of prayer. I found myself becoming closer with Mary, as I shared with her more of my life than ever before. She knew the young ladies I liked, the classes I hated, and my greatest hopes and fears for that day. These visits were the highlight of my evening. This time became less an opportunity to rest my body and more a time to rejuvenate my soul. Over time, I became more comfortable being a young practicing Catholic, unafraid to step outside the church and hang around the street with a friend.

Now, this is not the first time I have talked to statues. Praying in front of shrines was commonplace for me in less public church nooks or basement chapels. However, praying on a street corner was a more fearful endeavor for two reasons. First, it heightened my fear of expressing my faith publicly. Even now, as a nonpriest and the furthest from a theologian, I wonder if people will question why I'm writing a book for the religion section. Second, this outdoor encounter with the Mary statue resurrected a different kind of fear. This particular fear might be the common plight of those God-fearing, good Catholic school children like me (and my mother, as I would later discover). Our fear is that in the midst of a simple prayer in front of a Mary statue in some unassuming corner chapel, mid-recitation, sore knees and all, . . . Our Lady would begin to speak! It might be anything—a hello, a smile, a wink, a tear, a call to action. Whatever it might be, I knew that it would scare me near to death. Most people probably think this would be an amazing experience, like that of the children at Lourdes and Fatima, but it would terrify me. I never wanted it to happen, yet I thought there was always a chance it would. In the back of my mind, every time I pray in front of a statue, I am mustering an extra, concurrent prayer:

> Dear Mary or St. Francis, St. Joseph or Jesus, please bless my family, loved ones, help me to find grace and goodness in the world, and help me to do your good work. Lastly and least important, please do not physically manifest

yourself in this statue because a) I am not sure I'm the guy you want to be talking to; and b) I am not sure I can handle being spoken to in direct statue form. While it would make for a very interesting Loyola Press exclusive, I am willing to give that up to keep my heart calm and my pants dry. Amen.

The statues have never talked back, yet my conversations are by no means one-sided. I have tried to listen and figure out what God is saying to me as I show my faith to others, to keep on understanding the place of a twenty-something Catholic in this world. Those twilight evenings with Mary provided a renewal of public faith for me. I felt awakened to a new faithfulness, to an unabashedly bold yet subtle pride not only in who I was, but also *how* I was. For much of my adult life, I wore a crucifix inside my shirt. When someone sneezed on the bus, I never said, "God bless you." At a restaurant, I usually said grace privately if I said it at all and was struggling with how much I wanted to share. With each new reflective religious experience, I felt more compelled to publicly explore a faith journey—starting in a French château village, on my knees in a wheat field as church bells rang from a twelfth-century belfry.

2

incognito catholic

It was the perfect storm of happenstance for such a moment to occur. I was invited to attend a wedding in the Loire Valley of France, about four hours south of Paris. It was the kind of town that almost felt untouched by time and therefore was open to the possibility of sharing the past. I was sitting outside on a lawn chair, checking e-mails when I heard a clanging in the distance. As I heard the bells, I couldn't help but think of one of my favorite paintings, *The Angelus,* by Jean-François Millet, depicting a farm couple dropping the tools of their trade to publicly pray to God as the Angelus bells rang throughout the town. Centuries later, there I was in that same French countryside, eager to drop the new tools of the trade (a laptop computer and a smartphone) to pray as well. I had no business being in the wheat fields; in fact, I didn't even know whose wheat it was. Yet, as the bells rang I shut everything off, walked into the field next to me, and dropped to my knees. I became the man in the painting, and it was surreal.

It was a realization of my deep hope to participate in this traditional Catholic call to prayer. It was a way to hearken back to a tradition I'm glad still exists somewhere in this twenty-first-century world.

Filled with that Catholic zeal, heading home on the airplane, I decided it was about time that I was unapologetic about blessing myself and praying as the plane took off. Usually I say a Hail Mary in my head, but I wanted to do it properly this time. So I crossed myself, folded my hands, and closed my eyes in a very deliberate way. I was supremely enjoying the fact I was praying—undercover no more! Then it happened.

Whack! My head was throbbing. I quickly opened my eyes and unfolded my hands to find a laptop bag in my lap. I gazed upward to see an open overhead compartment with luggage flying everywhere. Three hours of applied ice and a big bump later, I was finally able to reflect on what had happened. The compartment somehow opened during takeoff, a laptop was dislodged and, of course, hit the only guy on the plane with his eyes shut, hands folded, praying for safety nonetheless. In many ways, I saw this as the Patron Saint of Humor giving me a good laugh, a touch of irony from Jesus. Perhaps this relatively harmless love tap on the head was even a way of reciprocating the many jokes I had shared with Mary around her street-side statue. Or maybe it's just the ingrained Catholic lens that finds meaning in the joys and sorrow, bops and lumps.

I suppose there are potential perils to living out our faith too much on our sleeve. I've gotten surprising looks from people on the bus after saying "God bless you" and always seem to create an awkward encounter with our waitress when she checks in with our table as we are saying grace. Part of me wants to stop and explain, but I think we're getting better at the "Ummm, yes, fresh ground pepper would be lovely, . . . from thy bounty through Christ, our Lord. Amen" routine. Another painting that comes to mind during these moments is Norman Rockwell's *Saying Grace*, which depicts onlookers staring in a perplexed manner at a family praying before they eat. The Christian experience in a secular world can be confusing.

A few years ago, my family followed signs to a "Mary Festival," thinking it must be *our* Mary. What we actually stumbled upon was a Wiccan celebration: a bazaar peddling potions, sorcery, and magic organized to benefit a Wiccan member named Mary. Another time, when my mother asked for "Madonna" Christmas stamps, she was told that there was not a stamp in honor of the singer. As I said, it's confusing for both the secular- and sacred-minded.

A public faith life may bruise your head. It can embarrass you, challenge you, and create large amounts of anxiety and fear—on buses, in restaurants, along roads, or in Wiccan barns filled with wands. This is even more difficult if you are twenty-seven and some of your friends look at *you* the way you looked at the Wiccan warlock selling toads. Yet, along with its bumps and bruises, toads and dirty looks, the key ingredients to having a public faith life still include generous heapings of joy and grace, love, wonder, and strength—the strength to sometimes do things you never thought you could do.

3

adventures with rosary beads

This past year, I participated in a triathlon. If you were in attendance, you may have confused my outfit for underwear and my brains for mush. A triathlon consists of a 1/4-mile swim in the ocean, 14-mile bike ride, and 3.1 mile run—consecutively, in the hot heat of a shadeless Saturday morning. I don't often subject my body to such pain, but this was an odd goal of mine. I wanted the glory of impressing my Wisconsin relatives with this fact. I also wanted to put on my résumé in the "other interests" section: TRIATHLETE. I wanted the free gear and the snazzy shirt. I wanted the water bottle and an athletic excuse for eating large bowls of fettuccine Alfredo the night before the event.

Yet, as with many other things that one wants, this did not come easily. The typical training schedule for a triathlon is roughly three months. On the night before the race, I had done nothing to prepare, except to register and plop down my $95 entry fee. The night before the race, as the creamy Alfredo sauce was participating in its own triathlon throughout my arteries, I said a little prayer, asking that maybe I would over-sleep. It would be a great excuse and a likely one; after all, the triathlon was forty miles away, and the race started at 8:00 a.m. To accommodate parking and warm-up, my alarm was set for 4:30 a.m. I clutched my plastic set of rosary beads from the Sacre-Coeur Basilica in Paris, France, and gingerly placed my head on the pillow. Sure enough, in fearful and curious antic-ipation, I found myself in the car at 4:42 a.m. en route to the Atlantic Ocean.

The next few hours were a blur, as I witnessed hundreds of incredibly fit triathletes performing stretches, warm-ups, and preparation that I can only assume was on the last page of their three-month training program. The race started, and I was like a child thrown into his first swimming pool. Adrena-line pushed me through the swim in less than fifteen minutes; then suddenly I found myself on my bike, hitting the two-mile marker. At the three-mile marker, the adrenaline, excitement, and magic of Alfredo sauce dissipated into a hot pavement of reality. My bicycle was built in 1975. My "triathlon clothes" were not "quick drying." My shoes were from high school cross-country meets, and one barely had a sole. I began think-ing about my *own* soul.

As I trudged along regrettably, I thought, *Though I haven't physically trained for this, I've been preparing spiritually for this my entire life. I'm Catholic. Suffering is second nature—fasting during Lent, silent recess for weeks in Catholic schools. You want to talk endurance? Job definitely could have biked twelve miles after a swim and not even complained. Jesus carried that cross a lot longer than my dinky run, and he did it all in sandals.*

As the miles slowly disappeared, I realized that my triathlon heroes were not athletes, but saints and biblical figures, who might wonder why anyone would actually participate in a triathlon. As I dismounted the bike and began the home-stretch run, my biblical reflection skills started to get cloudy. My inspiration in recalling the details of Job and Jesus was fading, so I transitioned into what I knew best and finished strong with some Hail Marys—forty-five, in fact, maybe more, but I think I lost my counting abilities toward the end. I feel confident I had prayed at least a rosary by the time I passed the finish line.

If you want to call this a modern-day parable, let the lesson be this: Fools who don't physically train for triathlons *can* compete in a triathlon if they have had decades of spiritual training. But be warned: spiritual strength and prayer do little in the healing of blistered feet and chaffing of areas I will not further discuss in this family-friendly book.

As painful as the race was, I realized that all of my "spiritual training" had prepared me for endurance and determination. I also realized that my Catholicism was ingrained in me.

It would be there for me as I stepped out of my comfort zone.

4

harvard faith

I am a firm believer in Catholic schools. So are my parents and theirs before them. I always thought that I would attend Catholic schools my entire life. And I did, with one notable exception. When I started the pursuit of my Master's degree at Harvard University, it was the first academic year in twenty consecutive years that I was not enrolled in a Catholic school. It was the first time that my classmates were not predominately Catholic. Crucifixes were not on the walls, and prayer was just not something most people did before a Harvard exam.

Surprisingly, some people were intrigued that I was "still Catholic" and wanted to know all about the Vatican, saints, and Opus Dei. Conversations usually included some reference or point of clarity to the *Da Vinci Code* or "why the pope hates birth control," and even one person asked me why I was still part of a misogynistic organization that is corrupt.

I was not used to this, and I guess I didn't expect it. To some degree, it reminded me of the time I first moved to Boston and told all my friends that the best Italian food in New England was at the Olive Garden restaurant. People thought I was crazy and asked me many follow-up questions as to why I thought Olive Garden was the best. I thought, *Who could resist a never-ending pasta bowl, warm breadsticks, unlimited soup, free refills on the sodas, and even Andes Mints that came with the check?* My family agreed with me, as did many of our friends and neighbors in western Massachusetts. I never had to convince *them* of Olive Garden's greatness. Yet at Harvard, some classmates didn't know about the Catholic Church—which I saw as a spiritual equivalent to unlimited soup, salad, and breadsticks.

When people heard about my allegiance to the Catholic faith, often the debate began. My Catholic faith was no longer the status quo; I was a novel minority in a sea of compassionate, yet intellectually driven individuals who didn't know why I still touched my forehead, heart, and shoulders, then crossed my fingers in front of me. There were moments when I thought I might lose my faith and times when my faith was weak; yet, at other times my faith was completely emboldened. I learned how to explain being a mid-twenties practicing Catholic around the intellectual beacon of Harvard. No longer just a good follower of the faith as I'd been at other schools, here I was an ambassador. And as I pored over the history of Catholics at Harvard, I realized just how far we've come.

In the early days of Harvard University, each year Harvard College sponsored a lecture against "popery." In 1765, the college lector prayed, "May this seminary of learning, may the people, ministers, and churches of New England ever be preserved from popish and all other pernicious errors." Three years later, Samuel Adams proclaimed that "the growth of Popery" posed an even greater threat than the hated Stamp Act. As late as 1772, the city of Boston specifically prohibited "Roman Catholicks [sic]" from practicing their religion because it was "subversive to society." *

As a young Catholic man, I wouldn't have had a chance of getting a Harvard education in those days. And I know that in the era of skepticism and mistrust of Catholics, I would have been maligned. Some anti-Catholic Bostonians even dumped a block of marble into the Potomac River because it was donated by the Vatican for the Washington Monument. With this perspective of history, I tried to listen to people's questions with an open mind and sincere heart.

I've attended schools started by Catholic immigrants in two different states because there were no other options for a Catholic education. And now here I was, every morning passing the statue of John Harvard as he looked out over a yard that was no longer "preserved from popish and pernicious errors." I thought about how far we had come, and how Catholic education has survived and thrived amid opposition, misunderstanding, and persecution. It was in my first few months at Harvard that I truly realized Catholics had come a long way, but that there was still much more to be done. It inspired me to take a leap of faith into a changing world.

---

* From *Boston Catholics: A History of the Church and Its People*, by Thomas H. O'Connor (Northeastern University Press, 1998).

5

the catholicTV
network

The first program of the Catholic Television Center of the
Archdiocese of Boston was produced on the morning of Jan-
uary 1, 1955, when then-Archbishop Richard J. Cushing celebrated a Pontifical Low Mass in studios near Kenmore Square
in Boston. They were equipped with three RCA cameras, the
Center produced live and tape-recorded programs, and it purchased time from local television stations to air the Sunday
Mass each week.

Roughly five decades later, the CatholicTV Network is
seen by over 12.5 million viewers across North America and
is streaming online across the world. I watched this channel
many a late night, mesmerized by how different its message
was from much of the rest of cable television. As I perused
this channel infrequently over the course of two years, I discovered that the programming seemed to be focused on two

demographics: old and young. Either you were praying the rosary with the Knights of Columbus, or you were watching a young priest use a green puppet to talk to toddlers about the Old Testament. Occasionally there would be programs for families, but what I found missing in my late night channel perusal was programming for *me*. Now, my demographic is small, but I feel it is rather important. We are no longer dragged to church by our parents. We are not going to church simply for the sake of baptizing our newborn. New careers are starting, metabolisms are slowing, and Sunday mornings just aren't what they used to be.

During my first year at Harvard, I was enrolled in a course called "Growing Up in a Media World." The class looked at the pro-social role of television and focused on the good uses of this medium. We studied the origins of Sesame Street and the role that television can play in both child and young adult development. I kept thinking back to CatholicTV and why a strong voice for my generation wasn't represented. Gandhi always said, "Be the change you wish to see in the world." I became curious about just what kind of voice would speak to me; naturally, I thought my own voice could suffice. I did a little digging and discovered that the studios for CatholicTV were right in my backyard.

With an academic class in which to frame my pursuits, I decided the opportunity could not be riper. Using the virtual equivalent of a cold call, I sent an e-mail to both the president and general manager of this network. I explained to them who I was and what I believed was needed. I had discovered that there was not nearly enough of the twenty-something's voice on CatholicTV. There was programming for the old, the young, the families, but very little for the college and post-college crowds.

A few days later, I got a response from the president of CatholicTV, Fr. Robert Reed, who said he would be available to meet with me in the coming weeks. I later learned that they receive hundreds of "pitches" each year for new shows or new programming. To me, this was not a pitch but an extension of my faith life, spirituality and religiosity manifesting in the form of a conversation I would be having in two weeks. I thought long and hard about how to make sure my voice would be heard.

I decided to show up with more than an idea, but an actual product. I had four concepts completed and ready to unveil.

- The first idea was called "Places to Pray." This would have the same look and feel of a restaurant show on the Food Network, but rather than visit and showcase great restaurants around Boston, I would showcase the hidden gems where prayer could take place. I had already scoped out old monasteries, shrines, and secret cemeteries around Boston. I would visit them, provide my audience with directions to get there, and prompt them on what prayers might be said at the specific places.
- My second idea was called "You Want to Be a What?" It would showcase the stories of the seminarians at Saint John's Seminary in Brighton, Massachusetts. I had many friends already in the seminary, and they had compelling stories about when they decided to become priests and how their families reacted. Essentially, it would showcase the myriad life stories and talent of the Boston

Archdiocese and show the less serious side of the future leaders of the Church.

- My third idea was a bit more grandiose, called "This Old House . . . of Worship." It was a play on words with the home improvement show "This Old House" and would go around the country, profiling former church properties that have been converted into other entities, from restaurants to condos. The show would discuss the challenges of converting a place of worship into a commercial or residential property, and showcase some of the details that remain the same in new usage. I saw much growth for this show as church properties were being sold off across the world, and the process of re-purposing the properties would be ongoing. Of course, I would be the host.

- My fourth and final idea was my personal favorite but least exciting in a pitch. The idea had no name, no catch, no impressive hook. It was literally just my own reflections on life. They would be humorous, pithy, and sharp. As I was putting this idea on paper, I realized that there really wasn't a proof of concept unless I actually made one. And so, with three "treatments and scripts" all typed up and put together, I asked a friend to help me film a little reflection of my time at the Mary statue. We took some shots of me as I was praying, biking, and walking around. I recorded a brief voice-over and turned it into a little two-minute movie.

Armed with my laptop, freshly combed hair, and some directions to get to CatholicTV, I was off to make my pitch. Google

Maps said that my trip would be twenty minutes from Cambridge, so I allowed for thirty minutes. I followed the directions and ended up at the supposed location of CatholicTV networks. However, there was no sign, no apparent entrance, and no people. There were no satellite dishes or any markers that a national television network was at the address. It was just an old, brick office building. My gut reaction was that I had typed in the wrong address, but another quick Google Map search kept pointing me to this location. I got out of the car and walked into the office building.

I saw a dentist, a law firm, and an insurance company—no CatholicTV. Surely, the whole network had not gone under in the two weeks since I had made my appointment. Wouldn't Fr. Reed have notified a potential "show pitcher" that, well, there is no more TV station? This crazy thought quickly passed, as fear now set in that I was at the wrong address. Technology had failed me, and I had exactly seven minutes to get to the actual CatholicTV.

When all else fails, obviously a son calls his mother. She had been to the studios before, and in my frantic state, I thought she could help. She said she knew where it was and that if I could get to the CVS drugstore, she could direct me from there. That's like saying to a man lost in the forest, "If you can find a pine tree, I can direct you out of the forest." The only company more ubiquitous in the Boston area than CVS was Starbucks Coffee. Five minutes passed, then ten, then twenty. I panicked and called the CatholicTV number, letting them know I was running a little late. I blamed it on traffic, which was a problem at that time. I also was too proud to 1) admit I had gotten bad directions, and 2) ask for good directions. Eventually, I found "the" CVS, and my mother's directions saved me from completely losing my temper and appointment.

I pulled up into the CatholicTV parking lot. I was sweaty, discombobulated, stressed, and disheveled both physically and emotionally. I straightened my tie, grabbed my laptop, and started walking toward the studio door. In ideal circumstances, I would be ten minutes early, have fresh chocolate chip cookies as gifts, and feel both charming and eloquent as I began my pitch. Instead, I was recovering from my frantic thirty-minute afternoon malfunction. I told the receptionist that I was here, and she paged both the president and general manager of my presence. She then said, "They'll be with you in a little bit. You'll have to wait." *Of course, I'll have to wait*, I thought. *After all, I may have just completely thrown off their entire afternoon, and now they're going to have to squeeze me in between other meetings.*

I sat in the waiting room, dejected and saddened by these circumstances and the impending looks I knew I would be getting from people who don't reward poor punctuality and sweaty, uncombed bangs with show deals. In those ten minutes, I think I squeezed in about twenty Hail Marys and a modified Act of Contrition. Perhaps if God could take pity on me, so would his servants in media. The two men eventually strolled into the room, and I was greeted with warm smiles, welcoming arms, and the new knowledge that the address I had previously visited was the home of CatholicTV . . . in the 1990s. I guess Google hadn't gotten the memo.

The meeting room was all windows. Broadcast awards covered the perimeter of the room. The chairs were as comfy as you would expect a television studio boardroom's chairs to be. After some brief introductions and pleasantries, I was given the floor. I wasn't sure what to lead with, maybe "This Old House . . . of Worship"? It was clever but was not a show easily thrown together or financed. "You Want to Be a What?" was good, but not completely original. So, instead of a concept or pitch, I went with a personal history lesson.

I told them all the recent experiences that had brought me to this meeting. I explained how there didn't seem to be a voice or a place for young Catholics like me, who were past college campus ministry but not really feeling part of a parish. At the end of my little lesson, I asked, "Can I show you how I might be able to help?" I opened my laptop and pressed the play button.

I showed them the reflection on my visits with Mary on a busy Boston street corner. It was a brief, spiritual, and slightly whimsical video essay. After two minutes, the general manager, Jay Fadden, told me he had chills. Fr. Reed agreed with misty eyes. Then Jay said, "If you let me, I will air this tomorrow!" With misty eyes and two handshakes, I now worked for CatholicTV.

6

hero worship

When I was growing up, I had some help in staying on the "right track." I have had many good people guide or inspire me. Many, of course, were ordinary but remarkable individuals such as my dad or a few teachers.

However, I also had some help from Hollywood.

Bing Crosby and Spencer Tracy played some of my favorite characters of all time in movies. Yes, I know these are strange, very old actors for me to call "favorite," but we watched a lot of old VHS movies at our house. No, I'm not referring to their popular movie roles in *White Christmas* or *Guess Who's Coming to Dinner?* Rather, I admire their movies in which their characters also happened to be priests. While other kids were rewatching Luke Skywalker summon the force, I was rewatching Fr. Flanagan from *Boys Town* defend his orphanage from gun-slinging bank robbers. In *The Bells of St. Mary's,* I watched Fr. O'Malley be so kind to his elderly pastor, and care for everyone else with such grace and quiet kindness. It made me cry every time. After the movies ended, I imagined our parish priests as the lead actors in the Sunday stories. More recently, my home parish just introduced a new priest. He could have come right out of the old-fashioned movies, playing a lovable priest with a heart of gold.

I remember his first day at our home parish. I was just like all the other people in my parish—sitting in the pew and watching, somewhat like a movie critic evaluating a new actor at the drama of the Mass.

Just imagine that you have a new priest or a new pastor at your parish, doing his first Sunday Mass. He is more than likely pretty excited, yet also nervous. There are loads of us in the pews watching him. We listen to see if he sings well (not a deal breaker, but good singing is easier on the ears). We assess how fast he walks down the aisle. We look at his posture and poise. Of course, we rate his homilies. Do they start with a joke? Does he read them, deliver from behind the pulpit, or is he a roving homilist? Most important, does he high-five the little kids in the pews as he processes out during the closing song? (I always loved that.) As I am walking down the communion line, I can veer off from the left line and receive communion in the less populated right line; but no, I want to scope him out up close, during arguably the most important part of the Mass. I want to see how he says it, where he puts the wafer (is he a placer or plopper or sticker?), and if he makes eye contact. There is a lot packed into those four important words: The Body of Christ, Amen.

Yet, as I say "Amen" in what I hope is an assured, reverent way, I realize that he's probably thinking much the same about us, his new parishioners. Perhaps he thinks, *These people seem nice. They sing better than my last parish. The altar boys wear sneakers, though—I'll have to change that. The stained glass could use some cleaning. And why is the lanky young man with horned-rimmed glasses eyeing me up all during Mass?* He probably did not wonder beyond that, nor entertain the idea that his imaginary internal thoughts would be surmised in a book someday.

Pastors do play an important role in the life of a parish. Young children look for smiles. Older people might look for comfort or understanding. And young adult Catholics want just a little nod, a little recognition that they are on the Catholic team, too.

We also look to our pastors as role models. They might not be Bings or Spencers, but they can set great examples. I think of Cardinal Timothy Dolan of New York, who jokes around on the set of the *Today Show* with the anchors, but who always maintains the dignity of his office. He uses Facebook and blogging and the sheer force of his personality to make a person happy to belong to the Catholic faith.

As I scan for new Catholic role models in media, I often find my options more limited because of history and some misconceptions. Catholicism doesn't always have a positive image—instead of Bing Crosby (Fr. O'Malley) singing "Too-Ra-Loo-Ra-Loo-Ra," we now hear of pedophiles or indecency.

That is an ugly chapter in the church's history, and those acts should be condemned. They say that it's the bad news that makes the headlines. Yet, I wonder if the mainstream media would ever be interested in capturing the good Catholic role models? Some are priests. Some are not. In most cases, they are not terribly visible in the media. Sure, Mother Teresa and Pope

John Paul II captured some front pages and headlines. However, the Catholic Church is really about the good and humble people who live out their faith and vocation daily.

I look to the humble, good nuns who taught me and my parents and my grandparents as fine role models. The Dominicans who taught me at Providence College had a profound effect on my faith and how I want to live my life. Beyond the religious orders, I watched my father load up our minivan with his tools and head over to our parish to fix the church boiler or repair something that had broken. He pretty much helped construct a new cafeteria in our parish school. Many weekday nights my mother told me that my father would pick me up from sports practice because he was already there, in the gym, fixing something. Over the years, I could not believe how much he did. People started to think that he worked there. From climbing up into the roof of the church to fix a ceiling fan to crawling through tiny holes in the church basement to piece together wires, he was like the church's Facilities angel. And he did all of this "for the honor and glory of God." That means he never took a cent from the parish.

My grandfather called church bingo numbers every Tuesday for more than two decades. He also served as a lector and passed the basket at his parish. He was one of the first eucharistic ministers in our diocese. My grandpa couldn't hit a nail with a hammer. However, he used his talents and time to give service and to show his family that it is important to volunteer and help out. I like using my talents with storytelling and video as my way of serving. I always thought I should make the *Bells of St. Mary's II* as a way to continue using my skills in the best way possible to help the church. And for a while, I also thought this meant becoming a priest, becoming the next Fr. Flanagan from *Boys Town* or manifesting myself as an actual Fr. O'Malley.

I have come to realize that my vocation will not lead me to life in a rectory. However, when I think of my father, I know there are different ways to be a father and a helper. He helped the church install new boilers and cooling systems that saved them thousands of dollars in energy costs. He is not a priest. Of course, as his son, I am glad he never became one. He is a different type of father. He is the face of the church as much as Bing or Spencer is. And it is because of him that I try to make a difference with my writing or video work. He taught me that it is important to use my skills to benefit others—including the faith I love.

He also taught me to play the harmonica.

7

a harmonica in church

They say that when you sing in church, it's like praying twice. Under this theory, I'm not sure if I'm actually doing anything when I sing, since my off-pitch warbling likely offsets the praying. I do not think that the praying twice formula works for me. I will say, I do love listening to good church music and often take to heart the message of the lyrics. As a young cross-bearer, timed with each refrain, I would "lift high the cross." And as I returned from communion, with my scary sixth-grade teacher sitting right behind me, I embraced the song "Be Not Afraid." I knew that my teacher was surely scowling at my sneakers resting on the kneelers and that she disapproved of my butt slumped on the pew while kneeling, but I was not afraid.

However, I never participated in any church music group as a youngster, unless you count the mandatory Christmas pageant at school. Also, I was a really good king at one Christmas Eve liturgy. A few years back, I joined St. Ignatius Parish in Chestnut Hill, Massachusetts. Someone would announce at the beginning of Mass, "If you have musical talents, we'd love to have you join our group. Talk to me after church." And for two years in the back of that church I thought, *I wonder if I'll ever have the guts to walk up to the sort of intimidating musical director and say, "Sir, I cannot sing. I have no formal training. I do not read music. And I know this is a church—but I play a mean harmonica."* In fact, during long homilies, my mind would occasionally wander and reflect on why I couldn't bring myself to share this unique musical talent. I came up with a few theories.

The first theory was that I honestly wasn't sure I had much talent. When he was growing up, my father was a huge Bob Dylan fan, and he would tend to mimic the Minnesotan folk singer on occasion, both with harmonica and guitar. He even could sing along with a raspy voice. When I was ten, my father bought me my own harmonica, and I happened to pick up a tune on the car ride home. Ever since then, I would pick up the occasional tune and through no means of comparison thought I was pretty good. Still, how good did one have to be to praise God in front of several hundred of the faithful?

In addition to my talent insecurities, I was intimidated. I wasn't concerned about the prospect of playing in front of hundreds of people; I was timid about the prospect of approaching the choir director. A clear virtuoso and natural talent, he ran his choir like a profitable business, and it showed. Each week the music was near perfect, thus adding to my worries of being the blemish on the otherwise perfect musical machine.

Once I identified these fears, I convinced myself that the worst-case scenario of rejection really wasn't that bad. I should just walk up to this man and state my claim. Well, I chickened out a bit and didn't talk to him; rather, I just e-mailed my interest to him. And this man wrote back, "I've never worked with a harmonica, but I'm willing to give it a go." Told to show up at church an hour before Mass, I would have my tryout. Practicing the night before to Christian music on YouTube, I packed my "harps" and was ready for my big day.

As you may have guessed, the musical director was a giant teddy bear and very kind to me. I puffed along to a few church songs in practice, and he seemed mildly impressed. I remember the first time a sweet, bent note of the harmonica permeated the great nave of our Gothic style church. Dancing off the ceiling with the guitar, bass, and flute, my music was present and a real gift. I felt incredibly full of grace, and when the director told me to play along for the 5:30 Mass that evening, I was in awe of the situation. Playing that night meant I could overcome internal obstacles. It broke down insecurities and almost more important, it meant I could contribute to the liturgy. It also was really good that I didn't have too much time to think about it before jumping into the group.

So, I became the harmonica player at church. If you have strict notions about church music—pre-Vatican Two-era—and you just fainted, I apologize. Being "the harmonica guy" from church over the past few years has brought me such great amounts of joy. It has brought so many positive experiences, from the people I've met to the music we've produced.

Now, not all memories have been fond ones. In fact, some harmonica moments I'd downright like to forget. One of the most powerful songs of the liturgy is often the communion hymn. It is sung or played as the congregation is reflecting upon receiving Jesus, and it is important for the music to reflect the moment. The instruments are part of the choir, and we receive communion first and then begin playing. On this particular evening, I had a solo during the musical introduction. I had to walk back briskly to my position right after communion and play within seconds of sitting down. What I didn't anticipate in my rookie year of church harmonica-ing was just how present Jesus would be in my music.

As the opening chords on the guitar were strummed, I licked my lips and blew into the five hole on a G harmonica. The note that emerged through the microphone and across the church was comparable to an asthmatic seagull, or a hoarse duck, or a sick horse. Animal metaphors aside, the harmonica seemed as if it had mysteriously malfunctioned or broken between the offertory hymn and the communion song. Under my breath, I muttered, "Jesus." Little did I know I was actually talking to him. As I examined my harmonica, quickly cleaning out the holes and inspecting the reeds, a very, very tiny piece of communion wafer slid out. In my haste to play after communion, I had not properly consumed the host and was now playing for Jesus, *with* Jesus. After the introduction and a quick, yet reverent consumption of the remaining host, I played again. The rest of the song went fine.

For the next two years, I enjoyed participating in the beauty of musical ministry. If singing in church is like a double prayer, then playing harmonica in church has to be triple! Through this ministry, I was finding Jesus everywhere.

8

my st. paul
moment

My drive home from the CatholicTV station was the literal opposite of the car ride there. I stopped at yellows, drove under the speed limit, and listened to classic rock rather than classical music. To bookend the afternoon jaunt across the Charles River, I also gave my mother another phone call. It was the second in the course of an hour and again, completely opposite in tone. "Mom, they liked it. They want to put one of my ideas on TV," I said. She replied, "Good, Matthew, that is wonderful." We chatted a bit more about my hopes for this outlet, and then I hung up the phone, pulled into my parking spot, and shut off the car engine. I am generally conditioned to pray when I need help. Like most people, I turn to God when in need. I also realize that sometimes amid the excitement of good news, prayer is overlooked. However, not this time.

I walked into my apartment, and suddenly everything seemed more visible. The light shining through the window came in three beams, reflecting off my mirror. *Infinity Trinity,* I thought. My creative juices were flowing, and I wondered if this would make a good title for a new segment. I closed my eyes and heard my toilet running. This led me to consider a video essay on: "The Gospel of 'John'" and other parables learned from a broken toilet. That really happened, and my real and spiritual worlds mixed together as I dealt with a plumbing problem *and* probed the depths of my soul for more video ideas.

The rest of the week, I began seeing God in everything, relating all aspects of life to my religion, and wondering if it took a cable show to make me experience God in so many different ways. Whatever I experienced was now potential material to reflect upon. Weeks after my initial meeting, I had produced many videos, and they became featured segments on CatholicTV's flagship talk show, *This Is the Day.* Usually after the guest interview, one of the hosts would throw to my segment and then discuss it.

These segments were then repurposed on the CatholicTV Web site and uploaded onto the CatholicTV iPhone app under the *Reflections* tab. There was truly some fantastic synergy in this melting pot of technology, storytelling, media, and marketing. After we had produced six or seven segments, these videos were finding an audience. My topics had a broad range. Some were serious, such as my tender encounter with a local security guard about his connection to the Haitian earthquake. Another was a bit more lighthearted, as I described how the priest thought I was a fourteen-year-old girl behind the confessional wall. (Quick side note: Confessing to the priest that your prepubescent voice belongs to the male gender is quite embarrassing. "Umm, excuse me, Father, I'm actually a boy" elicits a response that can only be summed up by "Oh.")

Even at Harvard I began looking for God and seeking out connections to the faith. There was a Technology, Innovation, and Education research conference coming up, and I decided to submit a proposal on finding God through media. The proposal was accepted, and I was asked to be the final presenter at the day-long event. Amid presenters talking about smartboards in classrooms and online tutoring software, I walked up to the podium with a PowerPoint presentation called "Viral Vatican." In many ways, this presentation was my debutante ball, my grand walk down the staircase, as there was no going back. In front of a crowd of peers in the storied Askwith Lecture Hall in Longfellow Hall on Appian Way in the heart of Harvard Square, I presented on the topic most near and dear to my heart.

I talked about my faith. I talked about the need for more people to share discussion on religion, faith, and God. I wondered about how some of these conversations motivated me to go beyond just talking to action. I showed research of CatholicTV shows geared toward age demographics. I encouraged people not to interpret this presentation as only a Catholic issue, but something all religion is facing in an increasingly secular world. I shared my CatholicTV story and identified formative evaluation on my work, my outreach.

As I continued with the presentation, I felt increasingly comfortable. In the past I've given speeches and talks during retreats, but usually in front of a small group of Catholics or mostly Christians, many of whom I knew. Initially nervous, with each PowerPoint slide and subject brought up, I became more calm and comfortable talking about my work. It is in these moments when I often feel the immeasurable graces of the Holy Spirit most present and become assured of God's love. It's like the Trinity is patting me on the back and saying, "Matthew, keep going. We're all proud of you up here. I'll continue to help you, but it will be in mysterious ways."

At the end of the presentation, a faculty member in the room stood up and said, "Matt, you probably don't know this, but the way the sun is coming in from the window and hitting your head, it should not surprise you right now that you have a perfectly distinct halo, and I think that is quite appropriate for your presentation." In the warm glow of this sinking Cambridge sun, I smiled, looked back at the burst of light hitting the back of the wall, thanked the crowd, and went back to my seat. That afternoon, the way I identified myself at Harvard had changed. I went from a Harvard student who was Catholic to a Catholic who was at Harvard. My hunger to pursue this work would only grow.

9

a day of rest?

I had been chasing a slice of pizza that I'd not been able to get off my mind and into my stomach. It was the kind of craving that I assume a pregnant woman gets; yet for me, a very not-pregnant man, I just needed this particular slice of pizza. It was not going to be an easy task. No, the slice is not from a corner street in Venice or a beloved establishment that has closed its doors. No, this slice of pizza is readily available yet complicated to order, because this slice of pizza is purveyed by a youth-targeted entertainment complex. It is an eclectic eating establishment known as Chuck E. Cheese's.

No joke, I really like the pizza from Chuck E. Cheese's. Yet, a childless twenty-seven-year-old grad student really has no place at this birthday party haven. I certainly did not fit into the target audience at this animatronic wonderland—this germ-filled child's arcade. At least that's what my friends have told me. "You'll be the creepy guy without the kids in the corner, gorging on mushroom pizza and staring dreamily toward the ball pit, having your loving, nostalgic stares completely misinterpreted."

For years, I listened and stayed away, but the craving never left, the itch was never scratched. I am not a man to remain unfulfilled, especially when I know deep in my heart, or stomach, that something is calling to me. Sure, it may take a lot of courage, but by golly, I was sick of waiting. So, on a rather unassuming Sunday, I just showed up. I plopped down in the back corner, ordered my pizza, and soaked it all in. I reveled in what was the same: the parmesan cheese graters, the aerated black circles on the dough, the cup of tokens, the skee ball, the whacking of moles, and the decor of this unique American invention. I also reflected upon what had changed, namely, my height, weight, and enjoyment of some of the rides. However, the overall experience, the familiarity, the recognition of the changes, was one I fully relished.

Driving home with my bouncy ball and parachute man prizes, I reflected on the experience. Sundays are good days to return to the familiar. I couldn't help but think that maybe my Sunday trip to Chuck E. Cheese's parallels in some ways the return of Catholics to church. They are getting out of their comfort zones and doing what they feel called to do, after a long wait. It reminded me of the two-year wait I gave the harmonica. It spoke to me about the many months I waited to get my slice of pizza. I pondered how often we have either accepted or passed on any given challenge or hurdle. It certainly is satisfying when these fears or longings can be overcome. For me, many such moments have happened on Sundays.

Sundays have played a significant role in my life. Perhaps it is connected to being Catholic. Perhaps it is because my family made the day special. For whatever reason, the Sabbath day has meant a lot to me. Looking back, it's clear that my most memorable days have been Sundays. I'm sure I have some fond memories from random Wednesdays, but I know Sunday better than any other day. It starts and ends the week. It tends to feel like the longest or shortest day of the week (depending upon homework due the next day). I even like how it sounds—the implied promise of sun on this day . . . SUNDAY.

One of my favorite Sunday observations was watching the basket being passed. I had made a few notes on this part of the service over the years:

- When little old ladies don't bring their purse, I see them fake it with an empty drop and mischievous smile.
- The ushers who smile back at kids to thank them for giving money are the best.
- If you try to slam-dunk the folded-up dollar bill into the basket and miss, yes, everyone looks at you and, yes, you should quit CYO basketball.
- There will come a time when even though your mother still gives you money to put in the basket, you realize that you now have to do the giving by yourself. You have practiced for years, been an apprentice of your parent's generosity, and now are proud to plop in (not dunk) your own folded-up bills. Generosity and charity are learned behaviors.

Beyond the collection, this day hosted the 3:00 p.m. Sunday dinner at my grandparents, where I began my love affair with mashed potatoes. It was a time when my family followed the advice of Mary Poppins to go fly a kite, and without question, would get it caught in a tree (which is not part of the song). There were many perennial Sunday TV shows that our family watched over the years: *Star Search*, *The Simpsons* (when I was older), and—yes, I feel that in this book I can safely divulge this—I was an avid fan of the Sunday night shows *Touched by an Angel* and *Murder, She Wrote*. (Clearly I was not part of their target demographic.)

But all of this aside, it is the ritual of this day—knowing what to expect from it, knowing what it will bring—that makes it so impressionable to me. It is why I remember it more than the others.

I guess you could say that Sundays meant faith and family to me. It also meant another aspect of my life.

It was on a Sunday that I joined a gang. We did not have guns and knives or drugs and tattoos; we had albs, ciboriums, corporals, cruets, pyxes, boats, and a really nice lavabo. These were the tools of the trade. I spent eight years walking the aisles and pews of Holy Cross Church as an altar server. They used to say that if you make a mistake on the altar, just bow and walk away. We lived the dream. We had first dibs on communion, the best seats in the house. You serve at a wedding, you make twenty bucks for going to church and witnessing the union of two people in God's love—not a bad deal! Oh, and the bells! It was my favorite part. It was a time for a true altar boy veteran to shine. Three firm, well-timed wrist flicks of the bells, then gently placed down and slid silently to your fellow altar server.

One day after the communion consecration, I slid the bells to my alphabetically matched and scheduled co-server. He looked at me and said, "No, I can't ring the bells." I thought, *Who doesn't want to ring the bells?* I didn't argue with the guy; two bell rings in one Mass was a rarity, and I was happy to oblige. Also, there wasn't much time to debate this as the liturgy progressed. After Mass as we de-albed, I said, "Seamus, why no bells? It is the booming voice of the altar server. It is our chance to shine!" He looked sadly at me and said that last week he gave those bells a good ring, and the darn handle broke off and the bells went flying across the altar. The priest had to stop mid-consecration to return them to him as he gingerly finished a lackluster second ringing during the wine. Poor guy, he felt he could never ring the bells again. I wonder if he probably has flashbacks every time he walks into a department store around Christmas time. And I am sure he will never volunteer to man a Salvation Army donation kettle.

Amid all the bell ringing, great meals, and fun television moments, one special Sunday memory is forever etched in my mind. It does not involve the Super Bowl, an awards show, or a stellar performance on the harmonica, but simply driving with my father around Milwaukee. My father's mother had esophageal cancer and took a turn for the worse. We flew out to Wisconsin immediately after hearing this news to be with her. She was in hospice care for the first two days after her release from the hospital. Her seven children and many grandchildren were beginning to say their good-byes. Sunday morning came around, and my father and I decided to go to an early 10:00 a.m. Mass at his childhood parish. I knew my grandmother did not have much time. However, we thought we had time for our Sunday ritual and that some prayers would help. I also thought it might be nice if someone could give her Holy Communion.

My grandmother converted to Catholicism when she married my grandfather. She kept going to her Catholic parish even after my grandfather died, and she helped serve food at a local soup kitchen. Her faith meant something to her.

She came home from the hospital late on a Friday, and here it was Sunday. A parish visit for communion had not been arranged yet. These were not the best of circumstances. Time was precious. We did not know the parish priest. We felt he would come but not until all of the Sunday Masses were done. We had no pyx, and there was very little time.

As I was walking down the aisle for communion, I panicked and thought about negotiating with the priest right then and there in the aisle for two wafers. However, it seemed easier if I just shared my communion host with my grandmother. And so, after accepting the wafer, I broke off a very little piece. I wasn't sure exactly where to put it that would be respectful and safe. I placed it in a Kleenex in my front shirt pocket. I thought it was the cleanest and most respectful place. It also happened to be closest to my heart. While not a pyx, it would have to do under these extraordinary circumstances. Riding home from the church, I was truly excited to provide this service for my grandmother, especially as a trained eucharistic minister.

About halfway home from church, my father got a phone call that his mother had passed away. The next ten minutes I sat there in silence with my father, as we both made our teary-eyed return home. This was the first time I had lost someone I was close to in over ten years, and the pain was starting to sink in. Tears quietly slid down my cheeks, and some streamed close to the pocket closest to my heart. In it, still, was the unde-livered host meant for my grandmother. I was both saddened and comforted in its presence, knowing that Jesus was in the car to comfort the Weber men. We made it home. I quietly consumed the host as the ambulance pulled into the driveway. We approached the body and said a prayer and our last good-bye on this indelibly etched Sunday. I was gripping my father's hand like never before.

It was the hand I had held as I crossed streets and walked to school. It also was the hand I held at another special time.

10

sweaty palms

The Our Father was for many years my favorite part of going to church. It was the cherry at the bottom of my Shirley Temple drink, the last hill home after a long bicycle ride. When I was little and everything seemed boring and my Cheerios stash was diminished or spilled under a kneeler, I knew the Our Father meant it was almost time to go home.

Home meant Sunday comics with warm double chocolate donuts. The ensuing post-prayer times also meant baseball games, getting out of church clothes, and togetherness. Yet in our family, that togetherness began at Mass. The Our Father meant it was time to hold hands. No matter what minor pew feuds were entangling the Weber family on any particular morning, the Our Father brought us back together—literally. For other families, you would think the sign of peace would be the natural moment to, well, make peace. But it was the Our Father that, like clockwork, connected us all in prayer. Grudges or minor squabbles diffused into the cathedral ceiling.

Growing up, we belonged to a church that did not necessarily encourage this hand-holding tradition, so I often found myself looking around the church, observing us to be the only finger-woven bunch. There was a time when this bothered me. After all, I was a little paranoid that people might think we had been holding hands the entire Mass. They might see us as some overly sweet family that was just very close. In my early teens, with the "cool kids" a few pews back, I was very self-conscious. Holding my dad's hand for a prolonged period in church did not seem like it would serve me well in the cafeteria on Monday.

I went through a few phases of coping with this. Most notably, I recall a time when I squeezed my sister's hand with each syllable uttered in the prayer. Another time, I played with my mother's engagement ring. I even tried to hide the fact that we were holding hands by squeezing in tightly, leaving no cracks between our torsos for onlookers behind. As I write this, I very quickly realize what an incredibly misguided youth I was—worried that countless parishioners were all interested in staring at our family, fixated on this foreign practice of church hand-holding.

Later on in life, I came to find that other parishes, unlike ours, were completely dedicated to hand-holding in church, often encouraging the entire community to join hands across the pews and pray together as one faith family (as long as swine flu and bird flu were in check). I enjoy these practices at churches, but now I often attend Mass by myself. I sit in a back pew with few people around me, and I have no hands to squeeze, no rings to twirl around, fingers to hide, or side torsos to squish. Through college and many years of attending daily Mass alone, I found this part of Mass (once my favorite part) to be quite lonely. I missed my father's rough hands, my mother's opals, even my little sister's annoyed glares as I squeezed her hand tightly with every syllable.

While lonely, I did come to know the Our Father better, as my attention was solely focused on the words rather than on the digit-related distractions. Sheepishly, I would raise my hands a little to get ready for a hand-hold, but drop them in defeat a minute later, relishing the old days when it meant something more and my family was not scattered throughout the country.

Then one particular day during the sign of peace, a friend of mine boldly attempted an "air high five" from across the church. I happily reciprocated, and our "air hands" likely met somewhere mid-altar. It was then I had my "eureka" moment. I suppose in church it should be called an "Alleluia" moment, since Isaac Newton and the pope never really saw eye-to-eye, and likely did not hold hands in church either. Regardless of the name, it gave me an idea—a new way to experience the Our Father and still include my family.

The following day the Our Father began, and I proudly lifted my hands on each side. My fingers were open and my eyes were closed. On my left and right I clenched firmly the hands of grandparents I have missed for decades. Generations of my Irish immigrant family members were with me in full spirit, participating in a church tradition with profound love. I chose a maternal grandparent for my right side and a paternal grandparent for my left. I was always sure to include one from each side of the family, because I never wanted angel envy or soul favoritism occurring in heaven.

Ironically, I probably looked goofier than I had ever looked before during this storied spoken prayer at church, but I had no care whatsoever and worried not about onlookers from behind. I was sharing in this prayer with those whom I loved, in some cases, someone I had never actually met. I was again with my family, and I have yet to let go.

11

the andy rooney of catholicTV

Delivering my weekly two-minute video segments to CatholicTV was not easy. I worked all day and was also taking graduate courses. I usually made the segments between the hours of 11:00 p.m. and 3:00 a.m., then drove them over to Watertown and left them on the doorstep of the studio offices. Sometimes I would do all this work, and the episode would not air. It could be frustrating, but when it eventually aired, it would be a joy.

The time leading up to the deadline was a bit challenging. A typical day of filming was as follows: 1) Get idea; 2) film images; 3) write voice-over; 4) record voice-over; 5) re-record voice-over; 6) edit; 7) find music; 8) export; 9) re-export; 10) package tape; 11) drive to CTV; 12) collapse. In many ways, it was my own personal Stations of the Cross.

Of all the things I did in my busy week, putting these segments together was one of the highlights. Unfortunately, with time restrictions and chronic writer's block, these pieces would be produced often out of necessity because I knew they were to air the next day. If I missed my deadline, the world wouldn't end, but my vision would go unfulfilled. For roughly four months I produced weekly or biweekly segments. I thought of them as snapshots of life, video portraitures, or spoken essays. These segments were becoming a staple of the weekly *This Is the Day* talk show, and I was pleased with how this collaboration had turned out. My passions in life are making films and helping the Catholic Church. If this wasn't a better marriage, I didn't know what was.

Then, sort of out of the blue, I received an e-mail from Jay Fadden, the general manager. He and Fr. Reed wondered if I could come in to talk with them. I wasn't entirely sure if this was a good thing or a bad thing; maybe they were going to phase out my segments, or perhaps the need just wasn't there.

We met in a different conference room this time, on the second floor. I was nervous and excited. I realized that this was only the second time I had met with them since I started my segments. I worked at night and dropped off my tapes under the cover of darkness, and they introduced the segments and talked about them. It's funny how a friendship can grow and blossom with very little human contact. They knew me from my video; I knew them from their talking about my video.

We sat down and chatted like old friends. Jay mentioned that he was enjoying the segments, and Fr. Reed agreed. They told me that they were looking to start a new show that would be a news magazine format—like a *60 Minutes* for Catholics.

Growing up, I had thought that *60 Minutes* was actually pretty boring, with one exception—I loved the final segment with the older man with the eyebrows talking candidly about something different each week. I remember thinking, *How is this man on TV? He is certainly not the kind of person you would expect to see on TV.* He was almost the kind of ordinary person you might encounter in a barbershop or at a diner. He was folksy, real, and authentic. I often thought about that word *authentic*. Authenticity is something that is hard to define but easy to recognize. Andy Rooney, both on TV and off TV, was authentic.

As the boardroom meeting progressed, the intention of this get-together was becoming clearer. Jay and Fr. Reed wondered if I would find a way to have my video essays become a weekly final segment on their new hallmark show *Clear Voice*. With the imagery of *60 Minutes* in my head and my natural admiration for Andy Rooney, I declared to them, "I would very much like to try to be the Andy Rooney of CatholicTV." They chuckled and said, "Let's give it a shot."

As part of the new show, I was expected to deliver something with what they referred to as a "studio look and feel." With that came some great news: no more 3:00 a.m. shoots. No more 4:00 a.m. drives to Watertown. No more late-night deliveries to studio front porches. No more worries about lighting and sound. No more anxiety about whether the music was royalty-free. No more fears of projects crashing at 2:00 in the morning. All I had to focus on was the writing—the essays themselves, the words.

I decided to call my new segment "A Word with Weber." And with much shorter eyebrows, more than fifty years his junior, a little less crabby, and making a lot less money, I set out to become the Andy Rooney of CatholicTV. Yes, this would elicit some ridicule from friends and coworkers (especially when a press release went out). But the whole world was now my inspiration; all experiences could be reflected upon, and my faith life could be examined.

The world was my neighborhood.

12

oh, who are the people in your neighborhood?

She is nearly bald and nearly 100 years old. Yet, when it comes to kneeling at Mass, she still chooses the hard floor over the soft kneelers.

He is just a little kid. He and his friends are playing Angry Birds on their cell phones as they walk by a church. He stops, takes off his hat, blesses himself, and then carries on.

I am constantly impressed with the simple expressions of one's faith life by the old and the young. In many ways, the young and old seem to have a lot in common when it comes to this. There is a purity to one's relationship to God at these ages, almost as if the clutter of jobs, mortgages, insurance, and life has generally cleared up or is yet to begin. This similarity between the young and the old is one of the more beautiful aspects of our church. It's a relationship that I always seem to observe in some form or another. This beautiful relationship manifested itself so well to me during my years at Providence College.

Prior to attending this college, I was not someone who went to daily Mass. And by no means was I then, nor am I now, a morning person. Yet, by some stroke of intelligent college programming, Providence College hosted a daily 9:00 p.m. Mass. It was a quiet time—no music. This was a new concept to me at age nineteen. We never experienced Mass late at night. And for many of us, Mass was something we had to attend with our family. My mother has always emphasized the importance of giving time to God. So, here I was at college, with no more parental supervision, no one dragging me to church or telling me I had to go. But at the end of a long day of classes, clubs, and camaraderie, I couldn't think of a better place to spend thirty minutes of my evening than at Mass.

Of course, Mass on a college campus is different from your average parish Mass. The homilies are geared toward a college-age congregation, and the Dominicans, the Order of Preachers, certainly know how to preach! It was good to relax each night and reflect on the day lived and the days ahead. (I guess that is a bit of a Jesuit examen mixed into the night.)

I started going to St. Dominic Chapel about my second week of classes. I showed up, and the lights were dim. The usual Sunday numbers of people were merely a fraction, yet there seemed to be this strong community. I scanned the pews for familiar faces and was surprised to find some attendees that didn't seem to be traditional college age. The man in front of me was half my size, a little person, with trendy glasses and a prayer book in his hands. He worked for a water treatment center, loved Latin, was a staunch conservative, and would give a small bow and no eye contact during the sign of peace. One row behind me (and always ten minutes late) was a feisty pair of redheads. They were identical twins and almost impossible to tell apart. They were also in their mid-eighties. One was a former teacher; the other was a former nurse. Three rows in front was a middle-aged man of Portuguese descent who worked for the women's ice hockey team. He had one of the best laughs this side of the Mason-Dixon and exuded kindness. These four individuals were all present at my first daily Mass. They were strangers, random attendees, and quite honestly, people I never thought I would see at a 9:00 p.m. college Mass.

But there was something special in this unique recipe of a small daily Mass congregation that wouldn't allow for strangers to *not* become friends. As Mass ended each night, it was almost impolite not to say good-bye to the usual crowd. Sometimes conversations were recaps of the great homilies; other times they were about dreading the rain that awaited us as we left the chapel. On nice nights several of us would chat outside the church for close to fifteen minutes. These chats led to common interests in Friendly's ice cream, to invitations to go for walks downtown, invitations to birthday parties, and an exchange of holiday Russian eggs before Easter.

The two elderly twin sisters often sat behind me. Now, if you sit in front of the same two people in church for any length of time, you're bound to get sized up. Apart from being judged on my singing ability and whether or not I put my feet on the kneeler, I had been literally "sized up" by these women. They agreed that I would fit into their deceased brother's clothes, which had seen the inside of a closet for the past ten years. One evening, after exchanging the sign of peace, I was asked to meet them in the parking lot by their car trunk after Mass. Such an invitation might sound like the beginning of a scary story told round the campfire, but I, too, had done some sizing up and determined these venerable twins to be kind and good. And I was curious to see what they might have waiting for me in the trunk of a car on a dark night.

What they had for me was the first suit of many, and thus began my relationship with Bill and his clothes. As a relatively skinny fellow, with long arms and short legs, I've learned that most clothes do not sit well on me, and I have to special-order some items. But after running back into the chapel bathroom to change, I was excited to see that my compatibility with Bill was nearly exact. Over the next few months, the generosity of the twin sisters continued. They would periodically invite me to their car trunk after Mass, and there would be a new round of apparel to try on and subsequently model for them in the parking lot.

It was in trying on these clothes that I was reminded of some of the consequences of not wearing any . . .

13

movie morality

The movie *Titanic* had just come out, and it was the biggest blockbuster of my lifetime. It was the talk around the lunch table, and some of the boys who had already seen it shared an interesting tidbit: there was a little bit of nudity. It was PG-13, but the lunch table report was that Kate Winslet is painted in the nude and "they show them." I had just turned thirteen and was interested in history, boats, and big films. I was also beginning to be interested in some of my female class-mates, so the news of this did pique my curiosity. The mind of a thirteen-year-old is an interesting study. The mind of a *Catholic* thirteen-year-old on anything related to sex is an even more complicated study. While the idea of watching this scene did excite me on many levels, I kept thinking that it was some-how wrong for me to look at a naked woman. Was it pornography? Would I be bad if I enjoyed looking at them? Should I look away? After all, they were not my wife's, so was this OK?

I remember lying in bed, praying to God for some help. When it came to this question, I really didn't know who to turn to for guidance. I would just be mortified if I asked my mother, "Mom, is it OK if I look at a naked woman in a movie?" I recalled seeing pictures of naked women at museums. For some reason, I didn't seem to think this was a sin—perhaps because I never found any of them attractive and didn't have a crush on them, like I had on Kate Winslet. Needless to say, I was feeling pretty conflicted.

Well, the day finally came when I went to see this movie. I was more nervous walking into the movie theater than I was taking the SATs or eventually going on a first date. I sat down, ate my popcorn, and dreaded when the scene would come, still uncertain about what to do. A few hours into the movie, Leonardo DiCaprio began painting, Kate Winslet's clothes came off, and I turned away immediately. I was proud of myself, yet I must say I was not entirely virtuous; my turn was but ninety degrees to the right, my eyes did not shut, and I decided that a blurred, barely visible, yet shape-recognizing, peripheral view of Ms. Winslet would be OK.

It was a happy middle ground, one of balance and hopeful integrity for a thirteen-year-old boy slowly becoming a man. Ironically, ten years later I would invite both my parents to see the Kate Winslet movie *The Reader*, which unbeknown to me (and my mortified parents) had several minutes of frontal nudity of Kate Winslet; we all blocked our peripheral vision and looked down in utter embarrassment. Perhaps this was God's delayed response to my quasi-virtuous, quasi-hormone-motivated half-look a decade earlier.

This little dilemma was a microcosm of the overall challenge of trying to be a good Catholic. It's not really about the nudity. I've since come to understand why great works of art—bare or dressed—are things of beauty. The real problem lies in knowing what voices to listen to. Do I listen to the lunch table? To the teaching of the church? To my parents? And now, as an adult, to whom do I listen?

14

back to harvard

I had a semester left at Harvard, and a few things had changed since I started there. At the beginning, I was not on TV, and I was shy talking about God in a space that generally isn't reserved for such discussions. In a way, I felt as if every day was now Ash Wednesday, a day when everyone knows you are Catholic. Generally, I don't like people knowing all the details of my life, but sometimes you make exceptions for the sake of what is important to you.

A perfect example of this kind of exception is that first day of Lent. I hate getting ink or dirt on my skin, and I don't like people touching my face. This quasi-phobia regarding dirt or face touching is not terribly helpful to a Catholic on Ash Wednesday. I remember sitting many a year in the back of the church, scouting the people who applied the ashes. I would scope out who used the least amount, and who refrained from pressing hard on the forehead with their thumb. I analyzed how often they reapplied and how they would deal with bangs.

Also, I was apprehensive about what to do with the ashes after I left the church. I really liked having them as a witness to my faith and the beginnings of Lent. However, between the ages of thirteen and seventeen, I had terrible skin, and the ash section on my forehead would always break out, leaving me with a heightened concentration of fresh acne in the form of a cross on my forehead. The subsequent days afterward I called "Pimple Thursday, Friday, and Saturday."

Luckily my skin has now cleared up, I'm OK with Ash Wednesday, and I sort of grew into my role as a known Catholic at Harvard. As I was wrapping up my final class, I thought it would make sense to connect these themes. I decided to unite all of them in a final project.

The name of my class was called "Informal Learning," and we were supposed to focus on an area that could be better served through some new medium of informal learning. I couldn't help but think that the field of religion needed this badly. In my months of trying to share the Catholic faith through TV, I realized it is difficult to share the nuances and true spirit of the faith. I then began to think about how other faiths represent themselves and to consider whether I had a true sense of how people of each faith self-identify. I thought that a multimedia digital platform that objectively and dynamically represented people of faith would be a fun way to cap off the year and my time at Harvard. This was a group project, however, so I needed to recruit a few more people to realize the importance of this work.

Later that week I submitted my proposal and asked if anyone would be interested in collaborating on this project. A group would be assigned to me, made up of people who mentioned they were interested. I was expecting tepid interest or no interest; working on a religion project in a tech/ed Harvard graduate class isn't the sexiest assignment. Yet, as it happened, three of the four members who were interested were Catholic, with our fourth member being a devout Christian. I had known two of these girls for the entire year, yet we had never discussed religion and faith. With this new academic space in which to discuss faith, our collaboration ended up being quite fruitful.

After class we would discuss our projects and then our faith. I started seeing them at church, and we even planned to have Mass in a classroom one day and invited other friends from across the campus to join. The Harvard chaplain came to one of the premier Harvard Graduate School of Education (HGSE) classrooms to hold a small Mass, in a circle of about ten HGSE students. In so many ways, my original perspective of Harvard as a secular place was transformed. From being made aware of Masses on different campuses to prayer groups and pasta dinners, I was amazed by the resources of the Harvard Catholic Chaplaincy and St. Paul's Parish. And now that religion was on the table, I was approached by people of other faiths who wanted to discuss their religion as well—how it compared to Catholicism and how our views on spirituality varied. It was this constant engagement that motivated the success of our project entitled "Resurrecting Religion: Religious Literacy in the Age of Ignorance." These are our objectives as set forth in the paper:

> The primary objective of our project will be to educate junior high school (7th–9th grade) students about the

basics of several of the world's major religions. Junior high school students are preparing to enter more diverse educational environments and thus have a greater need for ideological awareness, tolerance, and understanding of the world's many faiths. For a variety of reasons, these needs are not currently being met in public schools. In a recent survey, only one in ten public school students could name all five of the major world religions (Christianity, Judaism, Buddhism, Hinduism, and Islam); fifteen percent were unable to name any of them (Wachlin, 2005). Only 31% of teenagers could identify the sacred book of Islam (the Koran), and only 36% knew the significance of Ramadan (Wachlin, 2005). Students fared slightly better when asked about Christian facts. More than 80% of teens understood that Easter is associated with the resurrection of Jesus and could explain the historical significance of Moses (Wachlin, 2005). Still, over two-thirds of teens could not identify the Road to Damascus as the location of the apostle Paul's religious awakening (Wachlin, 2005).

Many teachers extol the usefulness of religious knowledge. In a survey of some of the top high school English teachers in the country, 90% said it was important for their students to be conversant in biblical facts. "I think from the standpoint of academic success, it is imperative that college-bound students be [biblically] literate. For the others, I think it's important for them to understand their own culture, just to be well-grounded citizens of the United States—to know where institutions and ideas come from," said one teacher (Wachlin, 2005). Therefore, we believe it is essential to reach children in the seventh, eighth, and ninth grades, in order to equip them with knowledge that will become useful later on in high school and in college.

It is important that such a project have clear, quantifiable objectives. As such, we believe that those who use our program should be able to accomplish the following after they are done:

- Be familiar with the external manifestations of religious practices. For example, have an understanding of why Muslim women cover their heads, or what it means when Jews say that they eat kosher, so that in public spaces and social interactions the users become more comfortable with expressions of religiosity of others different from them.
- Have knowledge of the origins and central stories of the five major religions.
- Be aware of the important events in the respective religious calendars and the meanings behind them, apart from the information that can be gathered through mainstream media and external cues. For example, the Easter holiday is associated with Easter eggs and Christmas with Santa Claus and shopping, Ramadan with fasting, and Passover with seders. These alone do not give any indication of the real meaning behind the events.
- Be comfortable with identifying and differentiating the places of worship of the five major religions and have sufficient knowledge of what is appropriate and not when entering those places of worship.
- Have a general understanding of the spirituality of adherents of the five major religions and be able to understand the different approaches of each.

- Recognize the importance of living, working, and studying together with people who come from different backgrounds and have the necessary tools to forge friendships and healthy relationships.

Our project was a huge success and was lauded as both necessary and important by media industry executives to whom we pitched the idea during our last class. My coauthors of the paper were also driven by this strong reaction and heartened to know that others deemed this important.

I was both overjoyed and excited by these successes and inspired to see other Catholics, Christians, and non-Christians coming together in a school I had once thought of as incredibly non-religious. Instead, I experienced a 180-degree shift in my perception of a non-Catholic school. I now saw it as an open community in which to share stories of faith, talk about religion, and improve society across the world.

15

small "c"

The shrill sound of a happy rooster woke me up. My jet-lagged eyes were surprised to be disturbed this early. I rolled off the couch, glanced up at the wall, and gazed at a picture of John Paul II. I slid on my trousers and headed for the kitchen. It was 8:00 a.m., and the day was already old for the Ros family on their potato farm in southern Poland.

I sat at the kitchen table and exchanged smiles with my host mother, Danushka. I was teaching English in the small town of Hoczew and was being hosted by Heinrich and Danushka and their two teenage daughters. They didn't speak English, and my Polish after two days in Poland was still "evolving." My host mother smiled again. (It was what we did during awkward silences.) Danushka left the room, and I could see her walk out to the barn next door. My host sister Joanna poured me some cereal and said, "We wait for Mama."

It was my second day as a guest of the Ros family and my first time in a country where people didn't speak English.

Being isolated by a language was more difficult than I had expected; my strengths of communication were in my spoken interactions with people. After a few minutes, I asked Joanna where her mother had gone. Joanna's response: "We wait for Mama." I didn't argue with her and continued to wait. A few minutes later, my host mother came out of the barn, holding a large white jar.

She plopped it on the kitchen table, and Joanna began to pour it into my cereal. It was warm milk (almost hot) from the cow that I could see in the barn outside the window. Typically, I don't like warm milk. I actually don't like whole milk or even that much milk on my cereal. In fact, when it comes to milk, I'm incredibly particular about the brand I buy. I check the expiration date, the information about how the milk was processed, and I'm fussy about how cold it must be. Sometimes, I will even chill a glass in the freezer so that my milk is perfectly cold. Yet as I watched steam rise from my cornflakes and as my host mother—with an equally warm smile—handed me a large metal spoon, I knew this summer would be more than interesting.

Living with a Catholic family in Poland was an experience I'll never forget. The Ros family were the salt of the earth, milking their cow most mornings and taking a fresh quart to the aging pastor who lived in the rectory across from their house. There were two priests for every village, the churches were packed, and the singing was loud. I noticed that some people did not receive communion. I asked my host sister why this was so, and she said, "Many people have done bad things, and they don't want to hurt Jesus." This statement forced me to reflect on the sacraments, their meaning, and my relationship with them. Were the Polish just more devout or too conservative?

Communion is something I've always considered an automatic part of church, not such a conscious choice. But these Polish Catholics got me thinking. I shared my thoughts with my younger sister, Elizabeth, and she offered this analogy. People sometimes treat communion like a goody bag at a birthday party—you collect your prize at the end of the celebration. She said that sometimes people don't think about what they are receiving and why. The Polish approach may not be the best for me, but perhaps the approach I'm used to is not serious enough—we probably need something in the middle.

Being in Poland gave me a more global view of our big, beautiful faith—what we often refer to as Catholicism with a small "c." Taking milk to the priest and delivering homemade cheese put parish giving in a whole new light. I observed that nightclubs were closed on Friday because that is when Jesus was crucified. I'm not talking about Good Friday but *all* Fridays. Poland had created a culture in which faith and service are part of everyday life. The excitement of being Catholic and the vivacity of this shared experience was beautiful to see. It reminded me that no matter how different we are, from language to country, there are some things that we have in common. We can relate to milk—warm or cold. We can connect with generosity. It is the spirit of the Olympics embodied—the way in which sports can unite us all.

16

nun volleyball

At least once a year, we would suit up. My pants had to be ironed and my tie was always clean. My hair was combed and deodorant generously applied. It was the one day on which my Sunday best was destined to get dirty. Usually my nice clothes were tolerable only for the event in which I was requested to wear them: baptisms, funerals, weddings, and graduations. They were the kind of clothes that never really saw much action. They were good for standing around in, but on this one day, they were put to the test. Before we left the house, my mom wouldn't even need to ask; I always had the balloons in my pocket—not just one, but usually ten to twelve, and they were already quality checked for holes or defects.

The car ride lasted about twenty-five minutes. First, my family stopped at our local favorite Friendly's restaurant and got two ice-cream sundaes as a special treat for the people we were visiting. I'm not sure if they were supposed to have them; I just remember that we sort of smuggled them in. Then we talked about the game. The game was balloon volleyball, and we were always the away team. Our opponents never came to us because our competitors were the cloistered Dominican nuns of the monastery of West Springfield, Massachusetts. I am not sure how this epic game ever started, but it had been going on for many years.

My mom says she thinks the first time was after we attended a Mass in memory of my grandmother. My grandpa was still alive, and we visited with two special nuns after the Mass. The mood was kind of gloomy as we talked about my mom's mom. Everyone was still pretty sad because it had been only a month since Grandma Martin had died.

I guess I just happened to have some old balloons in my pocket. (You really never know what you'll find in the pocket of an eight-year-old boy.) My mother says that I always have had a whimsical side, and I love games. I do know that the good Dominican nuns bring out the best in me. I don't know why or under what circumstances I felt compelled to blow up a balloon during an hour-long visit with two older nuns. Yet, amid the talking and remembering and perhaps a little crying, an air-filled balloon was produced.

As for how that one balloon in an old monastery evolved into an annual volleyball game, I don't remember. But the game is now as storied as the Harvard-Yale football game (at least in *our* memories). I suppose the natural setup of the room is already conducive to volleyball. Instead of a net, there is a small three-foot barrier that separates the nuns' quarters from the visitors' side. Also, the force of hitting a small balloon over a barrier is as easy for an eighty-year-old as it is for an eight-year-old. The balloon really can't travel too far, so quick feet, agility, and fast reflexes are not necessary to compete in this game. For all intents and purposes, the annual Dominican nuns versus Weber family balloon volleyball game was competitive and, as the nuns described it, "a real hoot."

On the drive home, I was always surprised at just how much fun I had with these elderly nuns. Visiting them made me think about how they fill their days, never leaving the building. I would go home from balloon volleyball to watch TV, do my homework, and go for a run. At the end of the day, I would pray. I remember asking my mother what the nuns did all day. She described how often they pray. They squeeze tasks and duties in between prayer. We, however, squeeze prayers in between our tasks and duties of the day.

I often compare my life with that of someone else at a different school or in a different job, even someone in a foreign country. The potato farmers in Poland were very different, but they woke up, went to work, had dinner, watched TV, and went to bed. This routine, with some variations, tends to be consistent with many of the people I've met.

However, with the Dominican nuns, their vocation—their "job"—is prayer. It's funny to think of praying as a job, with the daily earnings being put toward a spiritual bottom line. It parallels the life of a student, who spends the day accruing knowledge and searching for wisdom. At the end of the night, he's smarter and sleeps with a sense of intellectual satisfaction and accomplishment. For the cloistered nuns focused on prayer, it must be easy to sleep well at night, knowing that their work helped the souls of the faithfully departed, those sick on earth, and encouraged peace and joy in the world. Not a bad day's work.

17

thinking outside the church

In the time it has taken me to write this book, I have gained roughly fifteen pounds. I have not made the time for my usual workout routine. What I've missed most of all, in these past few months of being hunched over a computer screen, is exercise. People go to gyms to stay in prime physical shape. They go a few times a week, often with one big workout each week; they go because they want to feel good. Perhaps on some level this is also why people see psychologists. They may have issues and want to remain in good emotional shape. After talking with a professional, they feel better.

People make time for what is important. And it's good to make time for activities that keep the mind and body healthy.

I've discovered, though, that what is often most needed and least talked about is spiritual health. I wish people could look to religion or church the same way they look to a gym. If

I just ate a big cheeseburger and milkshake, my first thought is *I gotta go to the gym tomorrow.* Maybe I was just mean to my sister or was rude to my mother. My first thought is generally not *I gotta go to church tomorrow, or confession, or say some extra prayers.* Yet, on the occasion when my response *is* to do this, I almost always feel better and more spiritually healthy.

In some cases, the church becomes the wellness center for spiritual health as well as a place to physically go for help. This was quite clear right after the terrorist attacks on September 11, 2001. Springing up all over the country (and all over the world) were candlelight vigils and prayer services where people could pray for victims and lament the tragedy. On that day, I was a senior in high school, driving home from school, not knowing where to go to feel settled. Once I got home, our family was not at peace. We stared at the television set in shock and felt helpless and a little afraid. Mostly, we grieved for all who had lost loved ones. Later, we would make donations and send gifts to the sons of a New York City firefighter who lived but lost so many of his "brothers." But when it first happened, we responded in an automatic way that came from years of exercise.

We flocked to the church, along with hundreds of other parishioners. Our souls were nourished by the strength of the community. Our priest was like our personal trainer, and the pews and kneelers were like Nautilus equipment. We cried and we prayed.

And the coming together as a community, as a parish, did matter. My sister Kerry was away at college, and the lawn in front of the student center was packed for a candlelight prayer vigil. People needed to be together. It's not impossible to pray at home or to get in shape at home. I bought an ab roller once, and our family owns a NordicTrack, but their use can be quite infrequent. They are all competing with other chores and duties of the house, and it is sometimes good to retreat from the home and go to a place dedicated and devoted to one thing. At a gym, it's health. At a church, it's spiritual health. A soul is nourished with community and Christ, and we don't even have to break a sweat.

But that doesn't mean that a life of faith is easy or without doubts.

18

good god!

I would be lying if I told you I never had a crisis of faith. There are days when I seriously lose the faith. Well, maybe *lose* is a bad word; perhaps, *misplace* is a little better. And while I'm trying to find my faith again, many terrible thoughts run through my mind. I wonder if there is a God. I think, *When I die, is that it?* I worry that there is no heaven. Of course, on the bright side, if there's no heaven, then there is no hell.

I've often thought about these things more than you'd expect from a guy writing a book about being Catholic. When I was little, I posed the deep philosophical question: Are there cheese curls in heaven? These moments of doubt are not always initiated by devastating experiences, losses of life or fortunes. I'll just be sitting on a chairlift, skiing one day, look around, and think, *Well, I wonder if it's all true.* Or at dinner, eating penne pasta and tomato sauce, I'll stare at the garlic bread and completely zone out with an intense existential crisis, focusing on the tiny molecules that make up the enriched wheat flour that was part of the bread.

Most of the time, however, I'm comfortable with my faith and feel connected to God.

Usually, I can find God easily in the joys and blessings of life. After all, God is love, and that is so important and intrinsic to my spirituality. Also—and this may sound counter-intuitive—I can find God easily in the pain and struggle, the death and heartache of life. I explain the world's terrible acts by believing that God acquiesces to our free will. I see the face of God in the struggle and pain of so many people.

Death and life do not make me question God. It's the uninspired minutia of the day that consumes me. The chairlifts and the garlic breads, the folding of towels and the waiting in line that quite infrequently, but quite starkly, give me chills. If this has happened to you, distraction is likely the best medicine—at least, that's my experience. Rather than dwell on it and sink deeper and deeper into a terrifying abyss of despair, I linger a moment longer, then set aside my thoughts. I don't fight them or deny them, but just let them linger until the spiritual troops rally the forces. Sometimes it takes a while; other times it is much quicker. Maybe it comes in the form of a text message from my sister. It may be just another simple detail to the day, but it reminds me of familial love and the power of the sibling bond.

Something has occurred to me while typing on the computer.

Misspellings and typos are common when you write a lot. For instance, one common error I make, especially when answering e-mails, is capitalizing the first and second letters in the word *the* so that it looks like "THe." I don't find this to have any significant meaning. However, the other error I frequently make is one I interpret as a direct nudge from the man upstairs. I will try to type the word *good* but what shows up is *god.* I'll go back and fix it, adding an *o,* but then I will pause. Was this really a mistake? Was there a deeper meaning in typing *god* instead of *good*?

These mistakes tend to happen at 3:00 a.m., when I have a paper due the next day and have been typing for hours. These mistakes can show up in angry e-mails to family members or in long chapters of god . . . er, good Loyola Press books that hopefully are being enjoyed. Good becomes god when God is good to me through this subtle nudge, this "hello" that usually comes when I need a reminder that God is present, part of the routine of my daily work—work that occasionally requires late-night pizzas.

19

the wisdom
delivery guy

As a budding filmmaker in college, I was beginning to test the powers of the craft. After a few film courses on technique and history, I decided to attempt a short film in every cinematic genre: musicals, thrillers, dramas, comedies, documentaries, and even mockumentaries. I wrote my first (and last) musical during a long wait before the Easter Vigil that year. The Boy Scouts were having some trouble with the bonfire (what I mean is, the fire from which we lit candles for the vigil), and I happened to have a pencil and a few scraps of paper in my pocket, and I started writing. The script was about a Red Sox fan who has a Wizard of Oz-like experience and consists of a cast made up entirely of my family.

In terms of college filmmaking, I collaborated often with my friend Buddy Lambert, who loved suspense/thrillers. We made spoofs or satires of other films. When the horror film

Saw came out, we made a spoof called *Slice*, featuring a Burmese exchange student as the killer; it was filmed entirely in our dorm room bathroom in less than two hours. We also spoofed the new *Willy Wonka and the Chocolate Factory* movie, along with old favorites such as *Silence of the Lambs* and *Million Dollar Baby* (our version was called *Million Ruble Baby*—it took place in a very Rhode Island-looking Russia and was filmed strategically in the parking lot behind our dorm room). These videos brought us a lot of joy and were often aired on the Providence College television station. Filming was not only a fun, creative outlet but also provided a unique alternative to what many other students did (or drank) on the weekends.

One late night, after filming a scene from *Slice,* in which I graphically saw off my arm with a butter knife to save my friend from an evil Burmese assassin, I was editing the footage we had shot just that night. I was hungry and placed an order with a local, late-night pizza place. They told me it would be half an hour. I continued with my editing and lost track of time. I looked at the time on my computer and saw that it was nearly 2:15 a.m., and more than an hour had passed since I'd placed my pizza order (sometimes creative juices can overcome hunger when you're in the zone).

I was pretty upset about this and was about to call the pizza place to complain, but when I picked up the phone, I saw seven missed calls and three new voice mails. They were all from the driver, who sounded angrier with every message. He wanted to know why I wasn't picking up, and he informed me that he would have to pay for the pizza since he couldn't deliver it.

In addition to being mortified and hungry, I was now feeling pretty guilty. I thought about not calling back but realized that the right thing to do was to call and at least apologize for my inconsideration, with a secondary goal of possibly still getting my pizza. He picked up the phone on the first ring.

"Hi, it's Matt, the guy you've been trying to deliver the pizza to all night—sorry I didn't pick up." He proceeded to lecture me about how inconsiderate it was, the gas money he lost, and how rude it was of me to not respond. I apologized again and told him I would be happy to pay for the pizza if he happened to still have it, and if he would be coming back to the campus for another delivery.

"I'm already on the campus with another delivery. Be in front of your residence in five minutes, and I'll have your pizza. It will be a little cold." Then I wished I hadn't called—now I would have to actually face this guy, get lectured again, and have to endure mean looks and sarcastic remarks. I grabbed a twenty-dollar bill for my ten-dollar pizza, hoping the 100-percent tip would smooth things over.

I waited five minutes, ten minutes, going on fifteen, as the restitutional forces in the world found some balance. At the eighteen-minute marker, an old station wagon pulled up across the quad, and a man lunged out of it, carrying a cold box of eight beleaguered pizza slices. He walked with purpose, and he started right in berating me for completely ruining his night. Halfway across the quad, he began shaking his head, saying, "I can't believe I'm doing this . . . unbelievable." In my right hand I clutched Andrew Jackson, hoping he could help mediate this bit of 2:45 a.m. drama.

The man's pace quickened, but when he got closer, he stopped abruptly. The anger and spite in his eyes and face completely disappeared and were replaced with compassion and care. "Are you OK?" he uttered in the kindest of tones.

A bit confused, I looked down at myself. My shirt was soaked in blood. My arm was stained, my pants ripped, and my collar completely torn off. My hair was disheveled and splattered with blood as well. It looked as if I'd just gotten out of a crashed car or broken up a fight between two rabid dogs. The once angry, now concerned pizza delivery man was looking at a hungry filmmaker, who hours earlier had cut off his arm with a butter knife and then battled a Burmese assassin in order to save his friend. In the excitement of editing my first spoof thriller, I had forgotten to change out of the wardrobe and wipe off the fake blood. The delivery man asked if I was OK, and I told him it was likely a rough night for the both of us. I grabbed my cold pizza, and he took his ten-dollar tip with a smile.

It's amazing the range of human emotions one can experience in a short amount of time. People go from loving a movie to hating it. They are angry one minute and compassionate the next. They transition from being hungry to completely losing their appetites in just moments. We see a lot of this in films; the good guy turns out to be evil, or the evil guy is good at the end. I believe much of this revolves around the notion of redemption and how it can provide so many people with peace. The night of the bloody clothes and cold pizza elicited an unusual level of reflection on how people forgive and why. It taught me to be more forgiving. Perhaps in the future, I should just picture the object of my squabbles in a torn, once-white T-shirt covered in red food coloring and vegetable oil.

Yet not every one of my college movies involved fake blood and knife-wielding Burmese assassins.

20

the dominic code

As my style and craft evolved (dare I say matured?), I began to see film as a powerful technique for social change. I used film to document and tell stories. For instance, when an old hot-dog joint was close to going out of business, I decided to interview the people, proprietors, and patrons who frequent the place as my final project for a class. I used film as a starting point for conversations. I often requested to produce a film rather than write a paper for some of my classes (definitely, I did not do this for my Calculus II final). For my sociology class, I created a film called *I Just Need Some Space: Female Bathrooms in America*. It took a unique male perspective on the female bathroom, investigating the need and reasons behind couches and parlors, which made for bigger and nicer female bathrooms compared to male bathrooms. It was made tongue in cheek, but it started a nice dialogue across campus about potential inequalities between genders.

At the height of my prolific filmmaking, the film *The DaVinci Code* was released. People were up in arms about how it portrayed the Catholic Church, and lectures and seminars were being planned to discuss the validity of this movie's claims. A lot of folks weren't getting the point and seemed to believe the farcical nature of Dan Brown's claims. I thought that sometimes the best way to teach is with example. If I produced an equally crazy plotline and put it together with some occasional facts, then maybe people would learn to be more critical movie watchers.

I was a student at Providence College, which is the only school in the country run by Dominican friars. It's a wonderful school whose countless good Dominicans helped shape me to be the faith-filled man I am today. Steeped in this strong Dominican tradition of St. Thomas Aquinas, Catherine of Siena, and St. Albert the Great, I and a couple of friends decided to write and produce a short film called *The Dominic Code*.

Our movie mirrored Dan Brown's book, but instead of racing around the Vatican and Rome, looking for clues and anagrams, our set was Providence College. The plot focused on a guy and a girl seeking to find "a Dominican secret so dark, it could shake the foundation of the order." After several stops at various campus shrines, buildings, and chapels, our two heroes discover a book that is supposed to contain the secret. When they open it, they discover it is the original copy of Aquinas's *Summa Theologica*. Providence College is one of a few places in the world where Aquinas is a bit of a folk hero; he is the one who married faith and reason, providing the basis for the great tradition of Catholic intellectual thinking.

Once our hero (played by me, a much younger Tom Hanks-looking character) opens the book, he quickly realizes that the title page on this original copy lists the author as "Thomas Aquinas, SJ"—the SJ standing for the Society of Jesus, otherwise known as the Jesuits. The great reveal is that Aquinas, the pride and joy of the Dominican order, was in fact a member of the Jesuit order, a rival to Dominicans in the matter of higher education. Asked what I should do with this book, I simply answer, *Veritas*—Latin for "truth" and the motto of the order and the college.

Notwithstanding the gaping chronological error in this plotline (the Jesuits were not even founded until 300 years after Aquinas's death), the film delivered a message and a slight chuckle, too. *The Dominic Code* was received to great enjoyment at the Providence College Film Festival and had a week-long run on the PC TV station. Fellow Dominican friends enjoyed it and made sure to point out just how factually inaccurate it was that Aquinas could be a Jesuit—and made the point, also, that even if Aquinas had had an option, he still would have chosen the Dominicans. For me, it was a first taste of impactful storytelling through film. On a much smaller scale, it lampooned and satirized in the same way Stanley Kubrick's *Dr. Strangelove* treated the Cold War.

Sadly, *The Da Vinci Code* director Ron Howard did not decide to turn my film into a major blockbuster follow-up. Perhaps being a movie star was not in the cards, yet there was a day when I and thousands of others certainly felt like one.

21

graduation day

Men in top hats and tails were common, bow ties were preferable, and all gates, doors, and buildings were open. It was a city-wide celebration of sending forth. From what I was told, every graduation at Harvard had sun, and the campus was the Platonic form of beauty. I chatted with some professors and some recent alumni, and they all agreed: Harvard graduation day was idyllic!

My parents and both sisters were planning to attend, and my mother had already bought a hat. Reservations had been made at my favorite restaurant and my classes, finals, and projects had all been wrapped up and graded. Receiving a Harvard degree was truly the fulfillment of a dream, and of all the days I wanted to go perfectly, this was one of them.

I had become nostalgic about Harvard in the final weeks, attending every lecture, activity, and gathering that was available. I took the long route that went through historic Harvard Yard, watching the banners go up, chairs set out, and tents erected in preparation for that special Thursday. Nothing in my mind really compared with Harvard Yard. It was aesthetically beautiful, steeped in history, and just a really special place. The only other place I'd rather have my Harvard graduation would be at the Vatican—but that doesn't make any sense and is not terribly cost-effective for most students.

Now, if it rains on my wedding day, I don't think I will be upset. If it rains during my funeral, this is no problem. I've been to enough Red Sox rainouts that I can deal with a rainy day ball game. In high school I gave the graduation speech inside a dank old gym rather than outside in the beautiful (yet rainy) wooded area of the school grounds. But as it would happen, the week leading up to May 26, 2011, was one of the wettest in recent Massachusetts history. It rained continually for six straight days with almost no sun and little relief.

My parents and sisters arrived the day before my graduation, and in order to save money, they all bunked with me. They were in my bed and on air mattresses, and I was on the couch. I checked my smartphone to see the weather: across the board, looking like a weather-themed slot machine, were all suns! In a weird way, I was wondering if this experience was quite possibly the best moment of my life thus far. My parents were in the room next door; my sisters were feet from them. I was finishing a degree I really loved, and my future seemed ripe with excitement and happiness.

Maybe this is the point in the chapter when you are waiting for the "and then . . ." or the "But . . ." Maybe you are expecting it to rain or my degree to be revoked or my sister to break her hand clapping so hard for me. While I am sure that would make for greater interest or tragic irony, I must report truthfully and happily that the day of my Harvard graduation *was* perfect. The weather was beautiful, my family was awesome, no one broke an arm, Placido Domingo sang to Ruth Bader Ginsberg as an honorary degree recipient, and the fettuccine Alfredo at the restaurant afterward was delicious.

Yet, I wonder what I will remember many years from now. Likely, I'll remember what is captured in pictures or what my family recalls. What no one else knows—and this would be a minor side note in the grand history of Harvard—is that I wore my father's shoes. Luckily, we are the same size, but even if we weren't, I wanted to share this day with him. Because of all he'd done—from help with calculus homework in high school to the countless hours he worked to support our family—my father deserved to share in this day. We did not come from wealth or prominence. My father grew up working on a farm and went to community college before taking night classes at Marquette University. It was not common for people in his town to go to college, let alone to a four-year school. When I told him I got into Harvard, not only did he cry, but he also beamed! Frequently, he squeezed "My son goes to Harvard" into conversations. In so many ways, that degree was as much his as it was mine.

Once I put on my dad's shoes that beautiful May morning, I began to think about other ways to pay homage to the people who helped get me to this day. Suddenly my undershirt was not just an undershirt but a symbol of gratitude. I had to choose wisely. I went with my oversized "Holy Cross" gym uniform from my grade school. I thought it apropos that my first institution of education should get some credit at this, likely, my last institution of higher education. I didn't wear that shirt often; it had sentimental value, and I'd taken it with me from apartment to apartment.

With my shoes and shirt decided, I wanted to think of something special to pay homage to my mother and her help along the way. I was running a little late and began to panic that I would find nothing to wear in her honor. I looked around my closet for special pants, a dress shirt, a tie that struck me as something I could wear for my mom. Then I looked down and realized that I was still in my underwear—which she had purchased. Come to think of it, much of my underwear has been purchased by Mom. Whether for Christmas, birthdays, or just from random Costco shopping, I always seem to end up with perfectly sized, perfectly soft underwear. Today, at my Harvard graduation, my gray underpants were worn for my mother.

In my wallet, prearranged the day before, I had a Mary prayer card and a special guardian angel coin tucked behind my two-dollar bill. God, too, in this physical form, would be represented on my journey through the Yard, across the stage, and back home again. I suppose, in retrospect, the day may have been perfect even if the winds were howling and there was no fettuccine Alfredo on the horizon. I suppose a day is what you make it, and even the simplest things in life can have greater meaning if you feel so inclined to reflect on them.

As I crossed through the famed Harvard gates, I pulled out my smartphone. I was going to capture all of this through picture and video and have a video memory of this day! I looked around and saw many others doing the same. I began filming and realized that some events should not be experienced through the small glass lens of an iPhone screen. The magnanimity of a moment, while captured, cannot be translated fully to video—the smell of the Yard; the coolness of the morning air; the nonvisual senses that are lost when one's sole focus is to capture a nice shot for playback later. I decided to put away my phone and commit this day to the deepest recesses of my memory. It might be nice to have some footage, but I didn't want to miss the unique joy of feeling the moment.

After that glorious day, I have become a great proponent of soaking in a moment without the worry of technologically capturing it. At a recent Yo-Yo Ma concert, of the dozens of attendees in the front two rows, more than half were watching through their iPhone. Many were probably thinking, *I can't wait to post this to YouTube and Facebook.* I am all for YouTube and Facebook and yes, the post would likely garner 18 likes and 7 comments, including one from a cool uncle who rarely posts. But in the actual moment, something is lost. I think of Neil Armstrong on the moon, holding out his flipcam as he took that giant leap for mankind. I think of the pope walking out onto the great St. Peter's balcony, one hand waving, the other videotaping.

I have fallen prey to the "report paradox," in which I am more concerned with capturing the event than truly experiencing it or enjoying it. Ever since I began my "Word with Weber" segment, I have been surprised at how often I am inspired to turn any private or public moment into potential content for a future segment. When I am at home helping my father clean up fallen tree branches, I lug large branches over my back for long distances. Rather than complain or ache, I see a parallel between that moment and Jesus carrying the cross. I think, *Well, I don't think I'll ever go through exactly what Jesus did that day. I hope never to be whipped and crucified, but carrying this large tree limb does seem to be as close as I'll get.* I had my mother take pictures of me carrying the limb, and BOOM, there was a new segment on CatholicTV, entitled "Bearing Jesus' Cross . . . Literally."

Recently, I was sitting in my room and in kind of a bad mood. I was hot and tired, and my pants were too small, and I had a long day at work, and I could hear my broken toilet still running. It was making a constant whushing noise, as if the flush cycle had not finished. Now I directed all my anger and bad mood at that stupid broken toilet. I wanted to fix it but had tried in the past and it still did this, and I was so frustrated.

Too tired to exert another effort toward fixing the toilet, I lay on my bed, closed my eyes, and thought, *I need a break from all this. I wish I was out in the country in a cabin in the woods. A cool breeze and fresh smell of pine in the air; it would be so soothing.* I was imagining the comfort, the stress-free environment, even the soft babbling of a brook off in the distance. Then I opened my eyes, and the relaxing sound of the brook was once again the running of the toilet and the source of my frustration. I couldn't help smiling at this—I'd enjoyed a moment's comfort from my own broken toilet. I grabbed my laptop and began to write about how "whatever is causing you pain—a person, an idea, a toilet—in some changed way, can bring you peace." Then I went over to the toilet and took pictures for a future segment.

Even now, as I write a public book and have shared private stories throughout, some of which I haven't even shared with my family, I wonder what remains mine alone, perfectly private between me and God. What material doesn't make it into the book or the TV segments or the YouTube or Facebook pages? I often struggle with how much should be shared, when the right time is to share it, and what the purpose of sharing really is. Beyond that, what is worthy to be captured on film or in words, and what are our motives for capturing it? Am I experiencing life in order to write about it, and is something lost in the attempt to communicate the moment? This is not the first time I have been at a loss for answers.

22

i have your son

It was my first real job. While I had babysat before and weeded the neighbor's garden, this was the first job that actually involved my yet-to-be-found-useful social security number. My mother had told me that this strangely hyphenated numeric sequence would be more important when I got older. Sure enough, during our yearly month-long trip to Wisconsin for the summer, my cool older cousin offered me a work opportunity and a chance to use that nine-digit number.

"How would you like to work at the Major League Baseball All-Star game?" he asked. That year, Milwaukee's new Miller Park was hosting the summer classic. "Of course," I said. Baseball was one of my favorite sports, and being involved on the "inside" in any way would make this a memorable experience.

This job ended up giving me my first taste of the professional film industry. I would be what Hollywood calls a "production assistant" for the filmed pregame show on FOX. The glamour of Hollywood had come to Milwaukee, and I was part of the forthcoming movie (well . . . TV) magic. This was every teenager's dream. It was also a strong lesson in humility and learning the importance of words.

My four-day stint at Miller Park involved many important duties.

- Guarding a microphone in the middle of a large parking lot outside the stadium. There was a microphone set up there. I don't recall why it was there; all I knew was that I had to guard it.
- Driving the wardrobe people back to the hotel. Not only did I not know my way around Milwaukee, but also highway driving was a bit of a challenge. Global positioning systems were still evolving and did not necessarily provide the guidance I needed in these situations. I also had just gotten my license less than a year before, so this was a nerve-racking task.
- Babysitting dozens of grade-schoolers who volunteered to participate in a massive, choreographed dance involving light-up baseball bats and movie star Ray Liotta.

Now it was on this third duty that I learned a big lesson. My job was to make sure all the children returned their light-up plastic baseball bats and were picked up by a parent after the rehearsals. Things had gone smoothly for two days, but on the final day of synchronized bat waving, one of the parents did not show up. After waiting about twenty minutes, there I was standing next to a little boy who was waiting for his dad. This was quite different from babysitting a stationary microphone;

the little boy was looking anxious and tired, and the day was getting dark.

Now, we were at a point in our society where not everyone had a cell phone. Luckily for me, my parents had just gotten me one, and with this cellular device came responsibility. Generally, my mother told me to use it only in emergencies. I deemed this situation to be worthy of those coveted daytime minutes.

"Little boy, what is your phone number?" I asked.

He told me the number, and I punched it in. I was so caught up in the fact that I was using this cell phone and helping a little boy that in the excitement of the moment, I didn't put much thought into what I was going to say. I could usually think on my feet, but in this situation I did not pay due diligence in my phone call prep.

Someone picked up at the other end, and a woman's voice said hello. I panicked. *Just tell the woman that you're with . . . um, what's his name? Shoot, I never asked the kid's name.*

"I have your son," I said, in a tone and voice that came out a bit strong and slightly menacing. Suddenly there was panic on the other line; a frantic "What . . . who is this?" whimpered the voice. *Oh great, now she thinks I've abducted her son. In fact, I think the phrase "I have your son" is actually used in the trailer of the movie* Ransom, *about a young boy who is kidnapped. I need to de-escalate this situation ASAP. Calm the woman down. Put her at ease.*

"He is safe." *Shooot! How did I do this again? Another stupid, terribly clichéd statement from a kidnapper. And of course, while I was getting more nervous, so was my voice. The "he is safe" line came out smoothly, but almost in an overconfident way that would lead the mother to think I'm in control and that is that.*

"Oh my gosh, oh my gosh," I could hear her muttering on the other end of the line. I was muttering that myself in the back of my mind. Had I really just accidentally kidnapped a kid by poorly explaining a situation in the parking lot of a baseball stadium? I looked over at the kid with some hope that maybe he could provide some semblance of calmness. I don't think he knew what was going on. He was no longer scared, but he was perplexed with my sudden profuse sweating and rapid changes in voice.

I needed to nip this in the bud. The only natural next step was to let the woman talk to her son.

"You can talk to your son," I said, realizing that if I were a kidnapper, the conversation would last two seconds, and the next question would be where to drop off the sack of cash.

Obviously, I am not a kidnapper, but on that warm Milwaukee night, I learned the power and sequence of words and how things are said. As the young boy kept reassuring his mother that he was all right, I became acutely aware of our speech. Sometimes it's not what is said, but how it's said and when it's said. This is true from the words "I love you" to any Hail Mary you may recite on a daily basis.

When the father of this boy rolled up ten minutes later, I smiled and said nothing. He was giving me a strange look as if his wife had told him, "I think our son is with some weirdo. Go get him and stare down the guy who made the phone call." As they drove off, I learned that saying nothing may be the best option in certain situations.

23

guns and shamrocks

I have never killed any snakes or grown a beard or tended a shamrock farm on St. Patrick's Day. I've never consumed green beer or found a leprechaun. I usually don't even think about St. Patrick, except for a few seconds. I suppose this is what happens when a saint becomes commercialized. Poor St. Valentine has it even worse; the hype and marketing overwhelm our memory of the actual man.

However, on a recent St. Patrick's Day, the saint and I became, albeit briefly, better acquainted. I was walking home at 10:30 p.m., and off in the distance were two college-aged men, one walking toward me, the other one following him. They were not looking at each other, but one was saying loudly, "Just walk away . . . just walk away." It looked like they were in a fight, and as I began to cross their path, I looked over and there it was: a black shiny handgun, pointed up against the guy's side, as he was telling him to walk away. Now, I was born in Wisconsin (where it is legal to bring a concealed gun into church), but I grew up in Massachusetts, where guns were slightly more popular than the New York Yankees. I had fired a gun once and was absolutely impressed and terrified by its might and power. After my one time on the range, I decided to avoid guns as best I could.

Back to the dark street and two men with one gun: for the two seconds it took me to pass this scene, I had to make some decisions. Do I inquire, "Excuse me, gentlemen, is there anything I can do to de-escalate this altercation? I'm working on a master's degree at Harvard and feel that I might provide an impartial perspective on your respective and differing points of contentiousness."

Or, do I jump on the guy, pull back his thumb, kick the gun away, secure the safety, and hold the person down in a jujitsu move I learned in fourth grade, hoping his buddies do not subsequently pummel my brain in?

Or, do I just hold my breath, look straight ahead, and send up a very special and speedy prayer to St. Patrick on this his feast day?—asking him for forgiveness that prayers are most often said during times of need, but I am close to peeing my pants and do not want to see death or experience death on this the date of St. Patrick's death; imploring him to protect and defend us all; reminding him that while I have a German last name, I am more than 50 percent Irish and come from a long line of Brennans and Sheas and Martins, and that I rooted for Notre Dame every year until I went to Boston College, and I just really want to make it home safely.

I slowly walked by as if I didn't notice anything. Walking right by them on the sidewalk, I was trying to look tough like John Wayne, yet I doubt he ever panted heavily while tiptoeing. Once I cleared the perceived danger zone and made it by them without any involvement, I just took off. I ran and ran as fast and as far as I could until I was on the subway, corner seat next to the conductor, and safely traveling home. I went with this fleeing option, because it was not a robbery and there were no women and children involved. I decided that it might be simply late night drama with a hothead in some sort of machismo ego match with another likely intoxicated Cambridge resident.

On the subway ride home, with my heart still racing, I was reminded of death. I know death can happen at any moment. I bike, I drive, I eat cheeseburgers, I ski. But sometimes guns make that moment seem more real, and I guess prayer makes those moments safer. That evening I grew closer to St. Patrick and was reminded that maybe I should chat with him and God more often, hopefully under different circumstances next time.

I have prayed in different places—on street corners, in fields, and during triathlons. Still, the church calendar nudges us continually to reflect and pray. I can't help but think of St. Francis of Assisi on my birthday, October 4. And I like St. Joseph's Day because it reminds me of the good nuns who taught me, and of my father who does great carpentry and is the perfect father.

The start of a new year also makes me do some thinking and praying.

24

forgotten mini tapes

While Christmas is supposed to be merry, New Year's is described as happy.

Happy. Happy Birthday. Happy Holidays. Happy Meal. Oh, Happy Day. This word is part of America's fabric. We're in the pursuit of being happy. When I set out to make my New Year's resolutions this year, one of them was to be happier and to make other people's lives happier. And so the greeting "Happy New Year" I mean quite literally. I urge you, next time as you utter this phrase, to truly mean it. Be happy and make life happy. Let this simple greeting be your resolution. When someone asks, "What is your New Year's resolution?" say, "Happy New Year." In Laurel and Hardy fashion, they might say, "Happy New Year to you . . . but what is your resolution?" to which you will answer, "A Happy New Year." This could go on for a while, so please explain what you mean.

When I was a kid on this special day, I used to race up to my room after the Times Square ball had dropped, and I'd lock the door. As quietly as I could, I'd open up my secret locked drawer and pull out my tape recorder.

I used this tape recorder once a year. Into this device I deposited the impressions of my heart, attempting to reflect on the past 365 days and to forecast the coming twelve months. These tapes benchmark my growth in wisdom and are book-ends to the increments of my teenage into college years. Part tradition, part preservation, I suppose my motive for these tapes was to provide a living history for my grandchildren. I always loved watching home movies from my dad's youth, and I wanted to provide that same discovery for my future kin.

Even with the advent of new technologies, I still attempt to use the tape recorder. I imagine if the tape recorder and tapes are discovered by my grandchildren in the late 2040s, they will be forced to resurrect an old means of communication. Beyond what is said, I like to think of a little granddaughter beginning her mechanical engineering career by reassembling this antique piece of sound engineering (that is, a 1999 tape recorder). I like to think my grandson will be inspired as a sto-ryteller and realize the importance of reflection and the con-tinued need for oral tradition, especially among families. I like to think another grandchild will be exploratory and curious, perhaps the one who is looking through the antique furniture in the basement, only to find a small drawer with what looks to be cassettes and a black device that might just be connected.

I hope that it is these small moments that will be filed away in the grand portfolio of the Weber family lineage, sign-posting the kind of people we Webers strive to be.

As someone with no children, perhaps it is brash to be producing content for the children of my own yet-to-be-produced children. Perhaps it is strange to already hope that one of my granddaughters likes engineering and that my grandsons like treasure hunting. But I believe in a shared future. I pray not for the specifics of this future, but for the broad, smooth strokes of painted peace throughout the world. Each New Year, I consider continued life a blessing in the fragility of the natural world. New Year's is a day to celebrate our humanity, somehow not managing to break our lease with the earth. It is a day to hope for the future, to remember the past, and to be truly happy.

In addition to my resolution to be happy, I committed to a year of adventure. Under no circumstance did I think that this would involve impersonating a west Asian bovine.

25

yak vision

A few times a year I moonlight as a yak. Not just any yak, but Zak the Yak. He's sort of a mascot for an organization called Room to Read, where I volunteer. Room to Read builds libraries and promotes education across the world. This past year they had a Halloween-themed fund-raiser at a local bookstore.

When I showed up early to this children's bookstore in Concord, Massachusetts, I was just some guy who was going to help stuff goody bags and serve wine to parents. I was very ordinary, wore a maroon sweater, and hadn't shaved. As kids trickled into the store, their parents politely nodded and thanked me for handing their child a plastic bag and free pencil.

Midway through the event, I was given the nod and escorted up to the second floor. Lying in front of me was what looked like a buffalo-skin rug. Alas, it was the mascot costume, complete with hoof gloves, long tail, and protruding horns.

At six foot three inches, I was pushing the boundaries of this costume's elasticity and providing myself with a unique yak wedgie that I would just have to endure. I looked at myself in a mirror and did not see Matt Weber. When I put on that yak costume, I was Zak.

And being Zak the Yak in a room of thirty children meant a few things. When a giant yak walks down the stairs to an energetic group of children, results will vary.

- Fathers will yell, "Look, Timmy, look at the cow!" Staying in character, I will not correct him or explain the subtle differences between the two bovine cousins.
- Some little children will cry when you approach them. They will scream, and when you extend your furry two hoofs for a hug, they will scream louder. The fear in their eyes, while directed at Zak and not Matt, will still be hard personally to brush off.
- Some kids will love you, and they will love you so much that they will require multiple high fives and hand-shakes—er—hoofshakes, and they will need to pull your tail no fewer than ten to twenty times a minute.
- Children love when yaks dance. This is just a fact.
- When a little child looks to his father and says, "Daddy, is that real?" and the Daddy's response is "Why don't you ask him?" and the little child walks up to you, asking, "Excuse me, cow, are you real?"—the only natural response is to shrug your yak shoulders and proceed to distract with more dance.

And the last thing about being Zak the Yak is that it is hard to go back to being Matt the Weber.

As the event ended, I quietly disappeared up the stairs. I peeled the costume off my moist three layers of clothing and reentered the room, looking as if I had just been in the bookstore's secret private sauna. To the few kids left in the room, I was just some tall sweaty dude in a red sweater who smelled badly. There were no more high fives or crying eyes, no tail to pull or hoof to extend. No dance, no drama. I quietly went back to my table and helped clean up the parents' dirty wine glasses and the detritus of Teddy Grahams wrappers.

When you put on a costume or uniform or patch, it represents something. It's why Superman wears a cape and tights, why priests wear collars, nuns (at least some of them) wear habits, and even why Christians wear crucifixes. Sometimes these things remind you of the greater cause you are fighting for and working toward. For Zak, that's building libraries around the world and promoting the joy of reading. For Matt, it's actually the same as for Zak—not a bad role model, these yaks.

26

uncle jesus

I once sat next to an Irish woman on an airplane. After she found out I had roots in County Kerry, she chatted with me for the five-hour trip from Dublin to Boston. She shared with me one of her very impressive mid-Atlantic Ocean Irish nuggets of wisdom: "Matty me boy, let me tell you something about love. It is the itch around the heart that you just can't scratch."

Perhaps this is a common phrase in Ireland, or maybe she made it up. In my younger years, I never really thought too much about love. I knew that love was patient and kind, a type of story, all we need, in the time of cholera, cannot be bought, and the name of a shack. I had heard that C. S. Lewis identified four kinds of love. The Greeks wrote about it. And Paul, the apostle, was pretty sure it bears all things, believes all things, hopes all things, and endures all things.

Colloquially, I used this word a lot. As a youngster, before I fell asleep at night, I often pondered if I would wake up the next morning. You hear of people dying in their sleep, and I sometimes reflected on what my last words would have been. So, from my corner room, lying under three warm blankets and muffled through my retainer, I would scream out to my two sisters and parents trying to sleep, "I love my whole family." My last word, *family,* and my last verb, *love.* The requisite response would be "We love you, too." (Apparently they were comfortable with their possible last word being *too.*)

In our family, we often tell one another "I love you." We express our feelings quite a bit for an Irish family from New England.

Of course, the romantic notion of love comes up faithfully every Valentine's Day. I tend not to let a greeting card define love for me, but this holiday does its best to fully exploit the word. On Valentine's Day, love can take the form of chocolaty nougaty goodness, color-appropriate long-stemmed roses, or a French-inspired dinner that will include not just an esoteric appetizer of choice before the meal but also a tantalizing dessert medley. After the meal, St. Paul would likely tell the Corinthians, "Love is delicious, and prickly, and fragrant. . . . Love knows no credit limit, love hopes against immediate diabetes, and endures excessive caloric intake."

On one particular Valentine's Day, I didn't have any plans or special lady in my life. I thought of others who might be in my situation and wondered if this day was also difficult or strange for them. I decided to slightly alter the way the day was celebrated and e-mailed many of my old priest friends. Valentine's Day is usually not something they participate in, but I was hoping they would appreciate being recognized as a loved one to a person who cares deeply for them—the digital equivalent of a scream across the hallway to those I do love. I wondered how a priest or nun celebrated or experienced Valentine's Day. Since my aunt is a Sister of Saint Joseph, I decided to call her up and wish her a Happy Valentine's Day. She was grateful for the call, and it reminded me of a humorous conversation we had when I was much younger.

"Why do you wear that ring, Aunt Marie?" I asked, looking at the silver ring on her left hand.

"Well, Matt, it's my ring for being a nun."

"Oh, kinda like a wedding ring? Well then, who are you married to? Jesus?"

Aunt Marie smiled. "I guess you could say that."

I smiled. Then my mouth dropped. My aunt looked concerned.

"What's wrong, Matthew?" She sensed that my young mind was churning.

"Nothing, Aunt Marie. Nothing at all. I just realized something. If you're my aunt and you're married to Jesus, THEN JESUS IS MY UNCLE?"

Another smile. "Sure, Matt, I guess he is," she said.

"Wait!" My mind processed family-tree data at near-computer speed. "If you are married to Jesus, *but* you're also a Sister of Saint Joseph, based on these two proofs, does that mean you married your nephew?"

"Matthew, I love you, but you are nuts. . . . Now, go get me a water."

As I got her a drink from the refrigerator, I realized that while this was probably not entirely accurate, it was cool to have Jesus as Lord, Savior, and Uncle—truly Someone who loves *his* whole family, and shows it in the dearest of ways!

27

celebrity food

It was long since my near-perfect Thursday morning graduation in Harvard Yard. My degree was already framed (and according to my mother, "a smaller diploma than she expected"), and I was working ten-hour days in my new job as Harvard's New and Social Media Officer. Producer, writer, director, curator—I was blessed to find a job by which I could tell the stories of the school I had grown to love and embrace. Working for an alma mater that was so good to you is like working for an organization of the faith—to believe in the mission of an organization turns a job into a profession.

Every morning I would get up and head to the Harvard Graduate School of Education, where its mission is to help children and make our schools better. Every ounce of what I do supports that mission, and I am blessed to enjoy the leadership of our wonderful dean, who inspires me on a daily basis. I feel the same way whenever I head to CatholicTV to film a few episodes of "Word with Weber." My mission on those days is to produce a story that brings to light the beauty of the Catholic faith. Under the direct leadership of CatholicTV and the good priests, cardinals, and pope, I put my all into that mission. From religion to education, I have happily found ways that I feel best serve this world during my short time here. It is that love that makes it OK to work until 9:00 p.m. on a weekday, because often enough, my job doesn't really feel like work.

On one particular night, after locking the office door and making a quick stop at the convenience store for a chocolate chip cookie ice-cream sandwich, I began to walk home. And then I heard his voice.

It was that iconic Midwestern drawl with a hint of Canadian accent. It was that voice that initiated the busting of ghosts and blues sung with his brother. I knew it was actor/comedian Dan Aykroyd before I even saw him. I wondered why Mr. Aykroyd was walking around Harvard Square on a weeknight, so I decided to take the scenic route home and get a closer look at this cinematic hero of mine. As my gait increased, I found myself to be only a good stride behind my hero and his two companions.

Earlier, I wrote about our societal need to capture excitement through smartphones and cameras. Perhaps I decried it and said that one should live in the moment and make memories for oneself rather than satisfy the compulsion to record everything. This advice I often follow. Yet, one should always be able to make exceptions.

"Um, Mr. Aykroyd," I said in a tone I would describe as terrifyingly confident, or confidently terrified. He stopped, turned, and said, "Yes, son."

"I was wondering if I could have a picture with you."

"Of course," he said. He graciously stood beside me, arm on my shoulder, as I pulled out my smartphone.

I hit the button that usually takes a picture but I heard no clicking noise. Rather, it was the softer sounding *blonk* that a smartphone makes when it is recording.

"Umm, Mr. Aykroyd, I think it's actually doing video," I said.

Obviously unfazed by being filmed and also aware that I was unlikely to be paparazzi, he said, "Well, that's OK. . . . What's your name?"

Over the next thirty-seven seconds, Dan Aykroyd interviewed me on Brattle Street in Cambridge, Massachusetts. Questions were basic, the camera work was choppy, but the experience was unreal and wonderful. Here was a man who was off to see a movie with his daughter and still was happy to stop on an overcast night to talk with a Blues Brothers groupie. I was overcome by his generosity. This likely happens to him ten times a day and will likely happen to him ten times tomorrow. Yet, he took the time to chat with me.

Well, in my rule book, no good deed goes unrewarded. After we exchanged our good-byes and he introduced me to his daughter, I offered him the only thing I thought he might want (and I had) at that moment.

"Mr. Aykroyd, would you like one of these?" It was my wrapped chocolate chip cookie ice-cream sandwich, which was still in its plastic bag and did not look sketchy. I'm not sure I would have offered him an ice-cream cone that I had been licking, but I needed to thank him in some way.

Dan Aykroyd inspected the treat and accepted my offer, took the ice cream, and went along his business. I went back to the store, bought a new ice-cream treat, and headed home.

When people do something nice, I try to show my appreciation through a gift. Even as a young boy, whenever we had a good time with houseguests, I would run after them as they were leaving and try to give them a dollar. My mother says I recognized their generosity of spirit and tried to reciprocate.

As I told this story of Dan Aykroyd to my boss the next day, he told me I should write a blog about other celebrities to whom I have given food. Part of my job is to interview through our podcast The Harvard EdCast some of the guests that visit Harvard, and I began to reflect on this. To date, I have given the following:

- A yogurt parfait to former Florida governor Jeb Bush
- A dozen cookies to noted children's author Lois Lowry
- A bag of salty pretzels to Washington, D.C., mayor Adrian Fenty
- Fresh cherry tomatoes to Harvard president Drew Faust
- A strawberry smoothie to actress Ashley Judd
- Chocolate chip cookies to U.S. Secretary of Education Arne Duncan

While I wasn't certain it was blog worthy (or even now, book worthy), I guess I have a history of giving food to celebrities. Perhaps that one-dollar bill a boy gave at the end of a dinner party translates to "Thank you for your time. I truly appreciate your talking with me. Since you don't need a dollar, have this yogurt, or smoothie, or tomato."

Giving can sometimes be a challenge. It's difficult to know when to give, what to give, what is appropriate, or how often to give. Does the president of Harvard like cherry tomatoes? I don't know. Does Dan Aykroyd like ice cream? Probably. What I've found in many cases is that giving is more about the recognition of a moment. I like to give the words "thank-you" an extra bonus—of cookies, yogurt, or salty pretzels.

And more than food or money, I have found that when people give of themselves, that's the best. Our family met one children's author who seemed bored and tired as she met adoring fans. We still remember her crabbiness. Yet, my sister Elizabeth once wrote to children's author Tomie dePaola when she was young and got a personal note back from him. She recently met him at a book-signing, and he was gracious and giving. Kindnesses are always remembered, whether from celebrities, ordinary folks, or any spirits that go bump in the night.

28

haunted houses

I have always been afraid of ghosts. The kind of horror movies that truly scare me do not involve violence or zombies or vampires or murderers, but the spirits that haunt our world. My rational mind processes this fear with some hesitation. I believe in the soul and that after death, the soul leaves the body to venture to heaven or hell. However, in my weaker moments, I do let my mind think about the stories I have been told about spirits that haunt or roam. Those stories, especially the ones that are told well, seem to stick with me, and they become more present at 3:00 a.m. when you can't sleep—and when you've lived where I have lived.

A quick recap at some of the "haunted" spots I have lived.

1. Fennell Hall. At age eighteen I moved into my first haunted residence on the property of the former Charles V. Chapin Hospital, or City Hospital for Contagious Diseases. This hospital complex was

purchased by Providence College in the 1970s, which converted many of the properties into dorm rooms. I lived for four years in what is now called Fennell Hall, during which I heard stories of old patients and nurses walking the halls at night. There were also tunnels connecting all of the properties that were rumored to be haunted as well; many patients supposedly died in these tunnels from contagious and infectious diseases. My room during junior year was in the basement and abutted the opening to this now condemned tunnel system.

2. O'Connell House. After leaving the old Chapin Hospital, I moved into the former summer residence of the early twentieth-century Boston Cardinal William O'Connell. This old Tudor-style mansion had been donated to Boston College and turned into a student union in the early 1980s. Three graduate students managed this house and had apartments on the second floor. I was one of the house managers. As rumor has it, one of the former servants in the house hung herself from the rafters in the attic and was found with her dog licking her cold, dead feet. Legend is that the woman and her dog still roam the house, especially when the house is disturbed with any construction projects or big events. My room was on the second floor, right next to the attic door, which was padlocked shut. We were warned by college administrators, "Never go up there."

3. EF-Cenacle Sister Convent. After leaving the haunted cardinal's residence, I moved into the former Cenacle Convent across from St. John Seminary in Brighton. The Cenacle nuns had sold this property to a for-profit language school called EF, which employed six Americans to be resident advisors among the 400 foreign students who lived in this converted convent. I was one of these six advisors. The lore of this building was that there was an old nun, Sister Agnes, who walked up and down the fourth floor of the building, looking for her room and her fellows nuns. She was often spotted in the former site of the chapel (now a study hall), which also happened to be right next door to where I lived on the second floor.

Now, what does all this mean? One could posit that I've lived in old religious buildings that come with legend, myth, and lore. Watch any show on the History Channel or Travel Channel and you'll see someone spinning a yarn about ghosts in old buildings. As a fan of good stories, I seek out the anecdotal history of any building I live in and am intrigued by the mystery of any place. From ages eighteen to twenty-six, I've been either blessed or cursed with these stories because I've lived in these places. On many a night, yes, the notion of Sister Agnes hovering past my room in search of fellow nuns frightened me. And yes, I made sure my feet were always tucked tightly under my covers so that no ghost dog could lick them.

Living in a quasi-unreasonable fear of spirits a good portion of my young adulthood, I thought of ways to make these otherwise fearful situations less scary. For one thing, I always stayed busy so that my mind wouldn't have any time to linger on my frightening habitation. I also decided that if I saw the ghost dog, the hovering nun, or the old nurse, rather than seeing it as a terrifying moment, I should celebrate it. After all, such an event would be a pretty strong statement of an afterlife (albeit not the most exciting or attractive way to spend eternity), and I should take it as an opportunity to engage with or help the spirits.

I also decided that if this happened, I would not be afraid to talk about these stories. I decided to partner with my fears rather than run away from them. At all of these residences, I gave tours of the property and made sure to include the legend and lore associated with each house's respective ghost. I talked about them as being friendly caretakers rather than frightening ghouls. I tried to humanize them and even made a short film about the O'Connell House ghosts, with a full tour of the condemned attic.

Now I live in a boring old house. It has green vinyl siding and a small porch in front. The yard is average size, and there are two parking spots. I have two roommates and live across the street from a bakery. As I was reflecting on this chapter and lamenting the days of being both scared and excited at the slim chance of bumping into a ghost, I left my big boring house and walked down the street to get my hair cut. Small talk with the hairdresser eventually led to questions about what I do and where I live.

"I live in the house across from the bakery." I said.

"You mean the green one?" she asked.

"Yeah, you know it?"

"Sure, everyone does. We've all been in it."

I was confused. "You have?"

"Yup, that used to be the neighborhood funeral parlor."

I smiled. Here we go again.

29

brazilian mass

I overslept. I had missed my 11:00 a.m. Sunday Mass. This immediately put me into a panic. I began furiously to look for Masses online and was hoping to find one I could get to by noon. Yes, of course there were 5:00 p.m. Masses that night, but also a Patriots playoff game that afternoon. If I could make both work, that was my goal. The length of time it took a Google search to afford me this information was frustrating, but finally I found an available Mass. It was close by, at noon, but in Portuguese.

There are a few key points that will help this twenty-ninth chapter of the book to make sense. I don't speak Portuguese. In fact, I don't speak any other language well, and often I make a Lenten promise to learn a language. I pondered going to this service. I don't speak Portuguese, but I do know the Mass. And I thought, *You know what? I'm going to give this a try.*

It was just a quick bike ride over to St. Anthony's Church. I walked up the steps gingerly, without the same confidence

I'd have when entering a church with which I am familiar and using a language I know. St. Anthony is the patron saint of things that are lost; as I passed an image of him to enter the church, I asked "St. Tony" to help me find a home here on this Sunday morning. The moment I walked into the church, almost everyone seemed to be smiling. All those attending were with large families, appropriately dressed in their Sunday best, and the church was packed. Worship involved clapping and singing and laughing. The sign of peace lasted for close to two minutes, and the Mass ended with the priest asking people to come to the front for a special blessing if they had a new child or if they were new to the country.

During that hour, I didn't understand one word that was spoken, with the exception of maybe *Alleluia* and *Amen*. I didn't know anyone there. I sat in the back, and the message of the homily was a complete mystery. Yet the Mass was powerful! I felt God's spirit in that community, through song and smile, presence and prayer. It reminded me of living in Poland and Puerto Rico, where of all the things that were foreign to me, Mass in a completely different language seemed closest to home.

I thought about how God has many houses and many voices. And I realized that I'm lucky to be part of this big, universal Catholic faith. I reflected on how each church is essentially an outpost for the faith across the world. Countries have embassies; religions have local gatherings of their faith communities. No matter what the building looks like or what the language of the priest is, it is always clear that the Holy Spirit is present. From Creole to Vietnamese, a Mass in a foreign language can be an opportunity to connect and expand your understanding of the faith, to renew your confidence in walking up the steps of an unknown church into a place you can call home.

In fact, I decided to make this more of a habit than a by-product of necessity. It connected me to people and ideas that were both incredibly similar and remarkably different. It made me think back to that Harvard paper of providing religious literacy across the faiths. While it is important for a Muslim to understand the tenets of Christianity, I find it also necessary for an Irish Catholic to fully understand the nuances of a Brazilian service. While the universality of the church is in many ways uniform, there is so much variety and diversity just within the faith, whether you're in Boston or in the south of Belize.

30

prodigal cheez
balls

The pancakes from Ike's Restaurant in Enfield, Connecticut, were simply the fluffiest, tastiest pancakes I have ever enjoyed. Ike's Restaurant has recently closed.

The "Tortellini Lady" from Western Massachusetts made her own tortellini (hence her nickname). My mother would buy them in small plastic bags from her house, and they would be a dinnertime hit twice a month. The Tortellini Lady died some time ago.

Certain things in life are irrevocably gone and can never be replicated. For things that I love, I attempt to prevent these situations. When I heard that the show *Due South* (a CBS crime procedural about a Canadian Mountie teamed up with a Chicago cop) was suffering from bad ratings, I wanted to do my best to keep the show alive. I ran all over the house on Wednesday nights, turning every TV set to CBS and even plugging in old TVs, thinking that each TV that was running the show *Due South* would help ratings (little did I know that Nielsen ratings work very differently). My attempts to save the show were to no avail, but at least there was some satisfaction in the preparation and the fight.

The story of Planters Cheez Balls is quite different. One day they were here; the next, completely off the market.

A little backstory: Planters Cheez Balls appeared in a cylinder and had the perfect crunch-to-cheese ratio. They were fun to eat, easy to store, and deeply associated with many childhood lunches and evening snacks. Perhaps you remember this cylinder of deliciousness, but you didn't notice its abrupt passing. Well, finding some Planters Cheez Balls became, for me, like searching for the Bermuda Triangle, Amelia Earhart, or the great white whale.

"Mom, can you go to that old discount grocer and see if they have any cans of Cheez Balls?" I'd ask, in the hope that even a can of Cheez Balls a few years old would suffice. I loved them with a cold glass of skim milk; they were the predecessors to my goldfish crackers as "evening snack of choice." I did my due diligence in looking for Cheez Balls, always scoping out the low volume five-and-dime shops for an old case, searching for this edible cobweb-covered vestige from my childhood.

Years passed, I moved on to other snacks, and needless to say, hope was lost . . . and then came a trip to Belize. It was a surprise birthday present that brought me to the small village of Placencia on the southern coast of Belize, roughly eight hours from Boston via several planes of varying sizes. After some reading and beach meandering, I decided to explore the small village and stumbled into the Chinese-owned "Nang

Kee" supermarket. To paraphrase a line from Casablanca, of all the markets in all the villages in this plump world of ours, I stumbled into this one.

There they were.

I had to do a double take—I could not believe my eyes! My Cheez Balls from childhood—the prodigal balls—had returned, and all it took was four connecting flights and a scary cab ride to the Chinatown section of Placencia, Belize. It would be an overstatement to say I was overjoyed; it's more accurate to say I was thoroughly "joyed." After all, I had sat down my taste buds years ago and gently let them know that the Planters Cheez Balls had to "go to a farm" and would not return.

I was tempted to tear into them immediately and gorge on their sentimental flavor. I would close my eyes with each crunch and flashback to the roaring 1990s—DuckTales episodes, pogs, and always secretly wanting a Tamagotchi. Back to a time when high blood pressure wasn't a concern, a pot belly had yet to emerge, and the world seemed like a fairly safe and stable place: a time when "Iran" was the beginning of a sentence in which one moved swiftly, "Afghan" was the blanket on my grandmother's couch, "Iraq" was how I would prepare for each game of billiards.

Reflecting in the cab ride home, I realized that these Cheez Balls were more than just autolyzed yeast extract, buttermilk solids, and vitamin A palmitate. They were emblematic of anything lost and thought to be gone; of grandparents and innocence, simpler times, and carefree bike rides on warm summer nights down hills, with feet fully extended. These Cheez Balls were *childhood*, and I was honored with the opportunity to revisit and reclaim that which is often left to the past.

I recorded the opening of the cylinder. I looked into the tiny iris of the smartphone, making certain that my first bite was caught on tape, . . . as well as the disappointment. The Cheez Balls were different, or maybe I was different. It wasn't the grand reunion moment I'd been expecting whereby a flood of taste and memory rushed back to my mouth, mind, and heart.

It was a stale moment, in the great scheme of things, not even close to being significant. But then again, I had hyped it up in my mind. A letdown? Yes, but it was also an invitation to continue the quest to dark warehouses of old stores, where a memory, a taste, and hope can last forever.

In a way, my search for my snack connects me with one of my favorite literary characters: Don Quixote. He was a man on a mission, a journey. He encouraged those around him to "Dream the Impossible Dream" and to see the best in others. I am not spending my life just searching for yummy, cheese-flavored balls. I really do see my life as a journey with providence, and while enjoying Cheez Balls along the way, I hope to do some good . . . and perhaps prevent some roadkill.

31

rosary rescue and relocation

It was one of those nights—I just wanted to get home. The only thing between me and my bed was a four-mile bike ride. The wind chill was -5 degrees, I was wearing a brown ski mask, and my ride was a purple girl's bike that my sister had bought at a yard sale about a decade before.

I started my journey home from a solid day's work at Harvard and was beginning to get into a groove. Off in the distance was a small, brightly colored object lying in the middle of the road. I rode past it but got a quick glimpse—it looked like a set of rosary beads. I kept riding and then had a moment of guilt. I don't know if it is Catholic guilt or duty to that which I believe to be sacred, but I wasn't comfortable with rosary beads lying in the middle of the road. As I turned my bike around and forged backward into a typical New England wind gust, I thought that it is rare to see rosary beads these days, let alone to find them sprinkled in the streets. Perhaps I was mistaken and my return trip would lead me to just plain old beads. I waited for a break in the traffic and then darted for the beads in the middle of the road.

They were red, plastic, and of the rosary variety. I'm not accustomed to picking up things in the road, but the previous week I had picked a ten-dollar bill off the street with no problem. There was little if any monetary value to these cheap plastic rosary beads, but for me they were packed with history and symbolism. I thought back to my own set of rosary beads and my grandmother praying in the car on long trips to Maine. I thought of how she had a special small bag for her rosary and treated it with the greatest of care.

After a moment's hesitation, I snatched them up and considered them rescued. Rather than keep them, I decided to drop them off in front of a church on my ride home. I chuckled at that—why is it that whenever someone doesn't know what to do with something they don't want, they think, *Just drop it off on the stoop of the church. They'll figure it out?* I dangled the beads over my handlebars and continued homeward.

Rosary rescue and relocation does tend to build an appetite, and my cold, weary bones were hankering for a snack. I wanted to enjoy this snack in the warmth of my house, so I dropped by a convenience store to pick up a gallon of milk and some goldfish crackers. I walked into the store and caught a glimpse of myself in the mirror. I wore a ski mask and had my hands jammed in my pockets. I glanced over at the store clerk and gave him a friendly nod and hello, hoping to de-escalate any fears my appearance might be triggering.

With milk and snacks purchased, I headed on my way. There were about two miles left in the journey, including a slight hill upward, a busy rotary, the church at which I would leave the rosary, and a slight hill downward to my home. I hung the plastic bag on the handlebars and gripped tightly, feeling the straps getting thinner and thinner from the weight of the gallon of milk. Up the hill I went, safe and sound, avoiding speed bumps and potholes that might jeopardize the integrity of the plastic bag. Approaching the rotary, I now had to merge with three lanes of oncoming traffic and then merge out for my home stretch. The bag handles were getting smaller and tighter as I progressed through the rotary. Cars were whizzing around me, past me, almost through me. Getting hit was not an option, as I had milk to drink and rosary beads to deliver. I made it past the third road and finally to the approach downhill.

Then I noticed that the bag felt suddenly lighter. I looked down to a cold hand that firmly gripped the straps of what was once a plastic bag. Glancing backward, I saw my milk and goldfish crackers impersonating roadkill in the middle of the right lane. For the second time that night, I turned my bike around to retrieve that which I value and wanted to try to save. Like a cop inspecting a crime scene, I gingerly pulled up to the goldfish and saw that they were relatively unharmed. The box was dented, but as my mother would say, "That's why God made packaging." I quickly snatched up the goldfish and then went to assess the milk situation.

She was hit. Flat on her back in the bike lane was an injured gallon of milk, softly spraying a steady stream to the sky. It was as if someone had used a pencil to poke a hole in the gallon and then let the laws of gravity and pressure do their business. My initial thoughts were to block the hole with my hand. I was wearing gloves and also had a good quarter-mile bike ride home. This was not a viable option.

Assessing the location of the leak, I thought if I flipped the gallon upside down, the flow and stream of the leak would be minimized. With the goldfish lodged under my armpit, my left hand firmly gripping the handlebars, and my right arm balancing this hemorrhaging gallon of milk like an irresponsible man holding a peeing baby boy, I continued down the hill. Milk was splattering everywhere, mostly on my coat and face as the wind blew harder. I kept gliding down the hill and was approaching the church. I actually said out loud, "Rosary beads, I think I'm going to need you for the rest of the trip home."

So with beads riding the handlebars, I and my now squished goldfish and my exponentially less than gallon of milk coasted home. I jumped off the bike, opened the door, and ran the melancholy milk up to the sink as fast as I could. Pouring the remains into every available mug, cup, or bowl, I managed to save more than half of the original contents. I put tin foil around the tops and found spots for them in the refrigerator. Later than night, warming up beside the radiator, I never enjoyed a glass of milk more!

As for those red plastic beads, yes, the rosary still rides my handlebars. It serves as a reminder of what is worth saving, what is worth going back for. It also shows me that it is good to make an extra effort, whether with faith or with groceries. Or with one of the more difficult questions I've ever had to answer.

32

culturally catholic

"If the Vatican goes to war with America, who would you want to win?"

I was asked this question because I'd brought up the issue of whether I identified more with being a Catholic or being an American. I had been reflecting on the notion of cultural Catholicism and was examining my deep cultural roots in the faith. With many generations of Irish Catholics on my mother's side and a solid history of German and Polish Catholics on my father's side, I discovered that my ancestry was interwoven with religious tradition. Pierogis were eaten at church dinners, and my mother would carve a cross into the tops of each loaf of Irish bread she made. They were all interconnected.

However, I began to push this notion of identity a bit further as the ball got rolling and the slope became slippery. Was I more of a Cambridge resident or a New Englander? Was I more of a writer or a filmmaker? The questions kept going until I landed on the most difficult of them all: Did I identify more as a Catholic or an American? This one was tough. My family has been in America for several generations, and I am a firm believer in this country. I love our flag, and I always tear up when someone sings "God Bless America." I love our freedom, values, and the potential for this brave, wonderful country.

History tells me that when John Fitzgerald Kennedy ran for president, many folks questioned his loyalty to his country. They wondered if he would report first to the Vatican before considering what was best for America. I do not confuse our government with my parish, but my faith does matter.

I love being Catholic. So much so, that I've even agreed to write a book about it. You're actually reading it. (By the way, thank you for buying or borrowing it.) As you have discovered, I think about my faith every day. I pray, I go to church, and I am a firm believer in this church. St. Peter's Basilica is one of my favorite places in the entire world, and I'm fascinated by church history. Yet, American history is also quite gripping. In fact, I was an American Studies major in college, and I guess as these matrices began to form, I happened to observe many similarities between the two institutions. Both are big, both are diverse, both have many wonderful components—and many areas that need improvement. Both prefer male leadership, both have been rich, yet less so now, and both strive for noble values. I continued the thought experiment.

Am I more American than I am Irish? Absolutely. Am I more Catholic then I am Irish? Yes. It would be very easy to just say that my nationalism and my religion are completely different entities; apples and oranges, separation of church and state. Yet I was committed to making this decision thoughtfully and to give this answer due diligence.

I've been Catholic exactly the same number of years I've been American, and I value the Beatitudes and the Constitution. My religion is not just a percentage of who I am; it transcends all elements of my work, my body, and my thought. My patriotism also transcends all I do, but it does not necessarily dictate the way I live. I pursue life, liberty, and happiness. I pursue love, joy, and peace. All of these are not mutually exclusive; there are elements of Catholicism that are very American, and values of America that are very much Catholic. In a way, generations of immigrants to America have made their American experience a Catholic one. That is the beauty of our country—its hosting and incubating of people of all faiths to live and thrive. We have developed beyond just the melting pot, into a bustling commercial kitchen of pierogis, dumplings, and Irish soda bread production.

Due diligence was done. A few days of thought, conversation, and debate, and I formed my answer: I came to the nuanced conclusion that I am culturally American Catholic and proud of each institution's watermark on who I am today. On the subject of who I would side with if the Vatican went to war with the United States, it would be hard not to go with the army still carrying swords and wearing multicolored, Michelangelo-designed striped onesies. I'm referring, of course, to the Vatican's Swiss Guard. I could have used the protection of both the Guard and the Marines on the night I almost died.

33

salamander search

I used to love hunting for salamanders. Well, I suppose *hunting* is the wrong word. It was more of a tracking exercise, where I would roll over logs and hope to spot one before it crawled back into the ground. It was at Disney World that I became fascinated with salamanders. I was waiting in line at the water bubbler and happened to catch the boy in front of us splashing an object in the basin. I peeked around his shoulder and curiously spotted a boy about my age splashing water on a red salamander. Not only was the boy bathing his salamander in a Disney bubbler, but the salamander also had a leash tied around its neck with what looked like a long piece of thread. The boy was talking to him; they finished the bath and moved on.

I stood there dumbfounded. Why did this boy have a pet salamander? Where did he put it when he wasn't bathing it? Who would ever think to put a leash around a salamander's neck? How is this done? This was inhumane, fascinating, and strange. From that moment on, I became very interested in salamanders. To this day, when our family recalls our trip to Disney World, it is the "salamander in the bubbler on a leash story" that always emerges as a primary memory (likely, not what my parents had expected when they brought us to Disney World).

Upon out return home, I bought a National Audubon book on amphibians and began my research on where to find these slimy creatures.

"Salamanders can often be located underneath logs in the woods, especially after prolonged rain," the book said. I immediately ran outside and headed into our small patch of woods. There were many logs, but my search yielded many overturned trees yet zero salamanders. I would have to wait for rain.

A few days later I was visiting my friend's house a few miles down the road. He lived even deeper into the woods. As my mother dropped me off, she told me to make sure I was careful and to not catch a cold. "It's supposed to rain," she said.

According to John J. Audubon, my new equation could be tested: Woods + Rain = Salamanders.

Sure enough, the heavens opened up. We ate our grilled cheese sandwiches indoors and then headed into the woods. My friend's woods were right next to an abandoned gun powder factory that abutted a nature preserve. They were deep, seemingly endless, and most important, full of freshly reserved logs, stumps, downed branches, and wet ground. With my new rubber boots, I kicked the first log. An explosion of creepy crawlers and tiny moving things emerged. Not only were there millipedes and centipedes, beetles and ants, but also a pair of big, beautiful green salamanders. I stared at them in awe, imagined them as distant relatives to the Disney World pet, and then moved on. I was afraid to put the log back on top of them because I feared a steamroller situation for the salamanders. Once they crawled away, I would move the log gently back to its earthly groove.

Unbelievably, the book could not have been more correct. Like forty-niners during the Gold Rush, my friend, his little brother, and I conquered the forest one stump at a time and gained our slow introduction to the vast network of salamander condos, time-shares, and co-ops. Time and place seemed not even to matter as nature and man (well, more like adventurous boys) moved in harmony. Dozens of logs later, and a handful of salamanders both named and observed, we found ourselves near the old gun powder factory. This meant we had gone far enough, and it was time to turn around.

Off in the distance were rumblings of a motor. In the foreground, we kept amused by walking the muddy trails, our boots snapping with every suctioned step. The motor stopped. We continued onward, down the trail and around the bend.

Directly in our path was a boy. I vividly remember his sandy blond hair and medley of dirt and freckles on his face. He was sitting on a dirt bike with his helmet in his hands.

"Are you them?" he mumbled.

"Umm, no, I don't think so," I answered quickly, in a mutter.

"You don't have the stuff?" He seemed to refer to something that was urgent, at least for him.

"Have what? What are you talking about?" I was confused and still a little naive to the possible scenario we had stumbled into.

"Wait, you're not them . . . then why are you here? Why are you here? What are you guys doing?"

I furrowed my brow and said, "We're just looking for salamanders."

Another motor began rumbling off in the distance. The boy on the dirt bike stared at us with perhaps the same intensity and attention we had been giving our amphibious friends just minutes before.

The other motor in the background hummed closer and seemed to preoccupy our new acquaintance. What did he mean by "stuff"? Who did he mean by "them"? At this point in my life, I hadn't seen enough adult TV to put these pieces together. I finally figured out that this may in fact be some sort of drug exchange, or drug deal to use more common parlance. It dawned on me that I was likely mistaken to be the delivery person, and the dirt-bike boy was either the buyer or running the route.

By an absolutely bad stroke of luck (and this is true), our salamander sanctuary was also some sort of small-time drug ring or route. For the first time in my life, I actually felt in grave danger. You tend to always remember your first time, and this one was a doozie.

"Run," I said, motioning to my friend, and we just took off—in separate directions, off the trail, our little legs carrying us as fast as we could go. The dirt biker yelled, and his motor started up again. Luckily, we were in deep woods, thickly settled with small hills and ravines that give the runner a sporting chance when being chased by drug mule dirt bikers at twilight.

With the ground as wet as it was, and my boots being rubber, each step I made was audibly significant, so I opted for a good hiding spot. Near a bed of green ferns there was a broken down, hollowed-out tree. It looked nearly dead yet big enough for me to squeeze into. I quietly shimmied into the frame of the tree, held my breath, and closed my eyes. For just one second I thought, *Hmmm, I wonder if there are any salamanders in here.* But this amphibian infatuation was hastily put not on the back burner but completely off the stove. Now I just listened.

The hum of the dirt bikes would come and go. Boys' voices were loud, then soft . . . then loud, then quiet. Within the cold embrace of a stiff oak tree, I thought about death for the first time. I thought about having never kissed a girl or gone to college, or had a child of my own, let alone having stopped being a kid. Spiraling into a heightened sense of despair, I suddenly remembered a story I'd heard from my dad.

As he tells it:

> There was a man during World War II who was in a bunker with his battalion. Someone threw a grenade into the bunker and killed almost everyone, but he was spared. Quivering in the corner of a carved-out bunker, the man started to pray. He thought of his family, his wife, and coming home. He told God that while he is ready to die, he would much appreciate coming home alive to be with his family. He promised God in that bunker that if he somehow could get home, he would pray at the Stations of the Cross every day after daily Mass.
>
> "Matthew, do you know that old man who walks around the church at the end of every Mass? That's the man from the bunker. He's never forgotten his promise."

I was not in a bunker, and this was not World War II. The dirt bike kids probably didn't have guns, and if they did, going from dealing drugs to murdering someone is a big leap. Eyes still closed and the story still fresh in my mind, I asked God for a similar arrangement. I told him that for the next month, I would pray the Stations of the Cross at church if I, too, could just get home tonight. I felt bad not committing to the rest of my life, but I wanted to be realistic, and to a little boy, a month seems like ages. To signify this deal, I said it under my breath in the tree, crossed myself and folded my fingers as if I was shaking God's hand. I also decided to be better to my family, to always take care of them, and to love them always. Yes, melodramatic, but by this point in the book, probably not a huge surprise.

I then emerged slowly from the tree. Under the protection of God, committed to an ideal, and with an army of recently befriended salamanders throughout the woods, I was heading to safety. The trail was off-limits, but an overturned log now and again kept me aware of familiar terrain. Avoiding the main entrance and exit to the woods, I opted to circle around a big hill, only to find a small pond between me and safety. I slowly eased into the pond—I vividly remember this was the first time my wallet ever got wet—and waded through guck and mud and murk to get out to the main road. From there, I walked another four blocks to get back to my friend's house.

As I unpeeled my five dollar bills and reveled in the fact that the ink on wet currency does not run or smudge, I was welcomed into the house. My friend was huddled on the couch with a clean towel, and another towel beside him, for me.

"Sounds like you guys had an adventure in the woods. Regular Tom and Huck, I guess," said my friend's mother. I just agreed and took the towel. Later on, I couldn't decide whether to categorize this story as an adventuresome boyhood tale of danger and excitement, or as a terrifyingly scary moment where I was in true peril.

Now I've decided to file this story away in a different category. The fear and threat of the dirt bikers seems less vivid, and what I hold dear are those eternal moments in the tree. As the sun set on my childhood relationship with God, it rose brightly on a new morning, where there were Stations to be prayed, family to embrace, and salamanders to be left untouched from a time that seemed a million years past.

epilogue

Now that the world knows I peripherally peeked at a naked Kate Winslet in *Titanic* and accidentally kidnapped a young boy in Milwaukee, there's really no turning back. If you're reading this book, maybe you chuckled a bit. Perhaps you related to a story or two or have had a similar experience. I'm sure some of you think, "He should probably just stick with TV" (which may be true), or "The only Harvard grad I want to spend money to read about is Mark Zuckerberg . . . maybe I'll wait for *Fearing the Stigmata,* the movie."

After twenty-one years in Catholic schools, it seems that my mere two years at Harvard taught me more about religion than I could have ever imagined. The beauty about sharing my faith with those at Harvard was that often I experienced the beauty of religious reciprocity. I learned all about the Bahá'i faith, the Hindu faith, and Sikhism. I've met a lot of atheists and agnostics, and more fellow Catholics. Certainly since childhood, I have come a long way since once asking my mother what a "pistol-palian" was. She said, "Episcopalian, Matthew. It's Episcopalian, and they're like our religious cousins."

From the day I got lost heading to the CatholicTV studios until now, I have made more than eighty video essays and have been broadcast to 12.5 million homes more than eight times a week. I wonder sometimes if my mother hadn't picked up the phone when I called her in a panic, would I have found my way to CatholicTV studios or given up? I wonder if I had arrived on time what my presentation would have been like, and if the CatholicTV people might have passed on it. What if my bike route to Harvard had been a little quicker, but didn't pass a Mary statue? Perhaps if I drove a car, none of this would have happened.

And I think about why you bought this book. Was it the catchy title? Are you my sister Kerry? Is this a gift from your Catholic godmother who thinks it looks like a quick beach read?

This being my first book, my hope is that you feel satisfied and that you got your money's worth. My publisher would kill me if I offered a money-back guarantee, but I'm open to personal negotiation if you found it intolerably long-winded. Perhaps I could offer you some cherry tomatoes or a Dan Aykroyd-inspired ice-cream sandwich.

Over the past few months, writing a book about fearing the physical stigmata ironically has provided an experience similar to having the stigmata. Yes, the process at times can be painful, but I honestly mean this comparison in a different way. Writing about God in your life brings you closer in your relationship with God. Mining for memories deep within allows for the opportunity to both look at and feel what's truly inside one's self. This book brings those memories out to the world and permanently identifies my devotion and allegiance to my faith, on the record.

If I ever run for public office, people will know of my days as Zak the Yak and as a harmonica player in church. They will know of Cheez Balls and nun balloon volleyball. The takeaway will be, I hope, that I am more than a man of quirky stories and odd happenstance—that embedded in the marrow of each chapter is someone steeped in the traditions of Catholicism, and it is this ecosystem that guides my life's work and action.

I hope this book speaks to you and provides one small example of a guy who jumped out of the stands, put on a helmet, and played as hard as he could. It is more than just doing something, but also owning it and moving forward. There are perhaps a few answers scattered throughout these pages, but the hope is that the reading can spur more questions. My expertise is not in answering the big ones, but more so modeling some humorous, often incorrect ways to engage with the nuances of a faith life.

Fear not the stigmata. Be a good Catholic in whatever way you can, and take this charge with an adventuresome spirit. Reflect, write, dream, hope, and turn over a few logs from time to time.

acknowledgments

Special thanks to my friends at Harvard, CatholicTV, family, Eleanor O'Donnell, Joe Durepos, Fr. Robert Reed, Jay Fadden, Kevin Clarke, and all those who have helped bring this book to the world.

about the author

Matt Weber is a Harvard graduate. As a producer for *CatholicTV*, he hosts a weekly segment called *A Word with Weber*, which airs internationally to over 10 million viewers. He is a frequent contributor to the *Huffington Post*.